CAMPAIGN 376

BARENTS SEA 1942

The Battle for Russia's Arctic Lifeline

ANGUS KONSTAM

ILLUSTRATED BY ADAM TOOBY

Series editor Nikolai Bogdanovic

OSPREY PUBLISHING
Bloomsbury Publishing Plc
Kemp House, Chawley Park, Cumnor Hill, Oxford OX2 9PH, UK
29 Earlsfort Terrace, Dublin 2, Ireland
1385 Broadway, 5th Floor, New York, NY 10018, USA
E-mail: info@ospreypublishing.com
www.ospreypublishing.com

OSPREY is a trademark of Osprey Publishing Ltd

First published in Great Britain in 2022

A catalogue record for this book is available from the British Library.

ISBN: PB 9781472848451; eBook 9781472848314; ePDF 9781472848338;
XML 9781472848321

22 23 24 25 26 10 9 8 7 6 5 4 3 2 1

Maps by Bounford.com
3D BEVs by Paul Kime
Index by Alison Worthington
Typeset by PDQ Digital Media Solutions, Bungay, UK
Printed and bound in India by Replika Press Private Ltd.

Artist's note

Readers can learn more about the work of battlescene illustrator Adam
Tooby by visiting the following website: http://www.adamtooby.com/

Photographs

All the photographic images that appear in this work are from the
Stratford Archive.

Osprey Publishing supports the Woodland Trust, the UK's leading woodland
conservation charity.

To find out more about our authors and books visit
www.ospreypublishing.com. Here you will find extracts, author
interviews, details of forthcoming events and the option to sign up for
our newsletter.

Key to military symbols

FRONT COVER ILLUSTRATION:
The German cruiser *Admiral Hipper* engages the British destroyer
screen during the battle of the Barents Sea, 31 December 1942.
(Adam Tooby)

TITLE PAGE:
British destroyers in heavy seas on the convoy route through the
Arctic, on their way to Murmansk. (Stratford Archive)

CONTENTS

INTRODUCTION

The battle of the Barents Sea marked a major turning point in the naval war in European waters. Strangely though, this wasn't so much due to what happened during the battle than what happened afterwards. At the time, the hard-fought campaign being waged in Arctic waters was at its height. The Arctic convoys, which passed through the cold, dangerous waters of the Barents Sea, provided a vital, strategic lifeline that bound Hitler's enemies together in common cause. This maritime link between the Western Allies and the Soviet Union provided the beleaguered Soviets with much-needed tanks, aircraft and supplies, while it demonstrated a joint commitment to defeating the common enemy.

In the summer of 1942, the Germans had brutally dismembered Convoy PQ-17. As a result, after one more outbound convoy, further sailings were cancelled until the onset of winter. Then, it was hoped that the long hours of darkness combined with the seasonably atrocious weather conditions would screen the Arctic convoys from the Germans. This though, didn't take into account the huge German commitment to the campaign in terms of aircraft, U-boats and surface warships. So, when the convoys resumed, the Germans were ready to renew the fight.

By then, Nazi Germany and the Soviet Union were locked in a death struggle at Stalingrad, and so these convoys were more important than ever. In order to help their troops on the Eastern Front, the German Kriegsmarine

Allied merchant ships lying in the Kola Inlet, waiting their turn to unload their cargoes in Murmansk. The inlet was the gateway to the port, and despite its bleak appearance it was a welcome safe haven after the rigours of the voyage.

planned to strike a crippling blow to the Arctic convoys – one that would finally sever this all-important sea route. Codenamed Operation *Regenbogen* (*Rainbow*), this bold attack would involve some of the most powerful surface ships in the Kriegsmarine's northern battle group, and although the plan was created before the first winter convoys set sail, the operation could be readily adapted and implemented once a convoy was spotted. In the end, *Regenbogen* would involve an armoured cruiser, a heavy cruiser and six destroyers. When the attack finally took place, on New Year's Eve 1942, it came within an ace of success. However, standing between the Kriegsmarine and the vulnerable Convoy JW-51B were five destroyers, supported later by two light cruisers.

Despite being hopelessly outgunned, these Royal Navy warships put up such a spirited defence that the Germans were driven off. The battle of the Barents Sea was a real David and Goliath struggle, fought out amid snowstorms, in the darkness of the Arctic night. In the end, the Kriegsmarine was thwarted by little more than bravado, radar and a huge slice of luck. While much of this success was down to the aggression of the British naval commanders on the spot, the seeds of German failure had already been sown before the battle began. The German commander was hamstrung by cripplingly restrictive rules of engagement. Effectively, his superiors refused to let him risk his most powerful ships. So, when the battle began, he was forced to display a degree of caution which all but guaranteed the attack would be unsuccessful.

The battle itself was little more than a skirmish, but it was one that would have major strategic implications, both for the Kriegsmarine and for the future of the war. Afterwards, in his wrath, Hitler threatened to scrap the Kriegsmarine's surface fleet altogether. Hitler lost faith in the Kriegsmarine, and so after the battle it would be sidelined, and even tighter restrictions would be imposed on its commanders. For their part, their victory eased the pressure on the Western Allies, allowing them to go over onto the offensive in the Arctic. It also safeguarded the flow of supplies between the Western Allies and the Soviet Union, which, ultimately, played an important part in the ability of the Soviets to drive back the German invaders, and then, finally, to end the war. These were world-changing consequences for a small, half-forgotten naval battle, fought out in the freezing waters beyond the Arctic Circle, on the last day of 1942.

ORIGINS OF THE CAMPAIGN

At 01.35 on Sunday 22 June 1941, the Germans invaded the Soviet Union. This attack, codenamed Operation *Barbarossa*, was the largest military operation in history. Attacking on a front stretching from the Baltic to the Black Sea, the German army and its Axis allies overran the Soviet border defences and began pushing eastwards. The Soviets had been wholly unprepared for the titanic scale of this offensive, and their defences were swept away by the German blitzkrieg. Within eight weeks, the Baltic States had been completely overrun, together with Belorussia (Belarus) and great swathes of the Ukraine. The key cities of Narva, Smolensk and Minsk had fallen, and the panzers were now driving on Leningrad and Kiev. Worst of all, by the end of the year, the Soviets had lost over 20,000 aircraft and

The strategic situation in the Arctic, December 1942

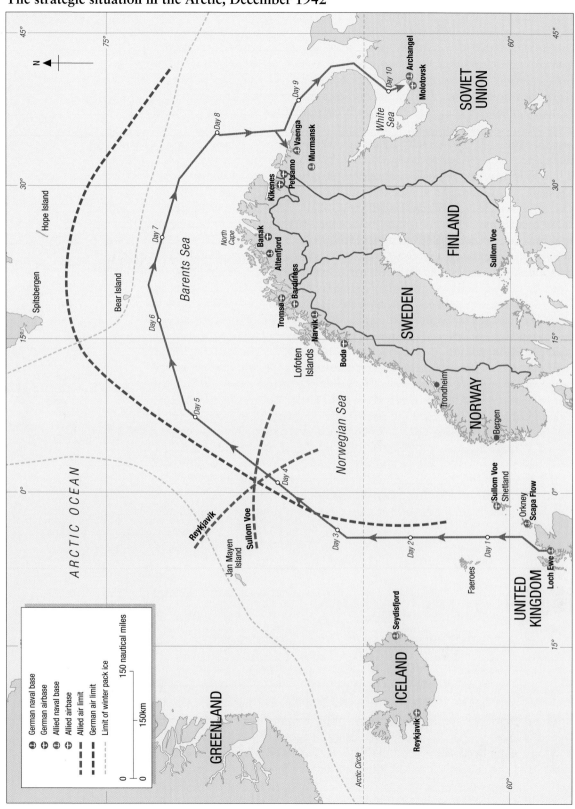

20,000 tanks. The 3.5 million soldiers killed or captured could be replaced more readily than this military hardware.

Consequently, Joseph Stalin began demanding help from Britain. For all his misgivings of the Soviet Union, Prime Minister Winston Churchill responded favourably. After all, the Soviet Union was now Britain's only active ally, and if Soviet resistance collapsed, the German war machine would then be free to invade Britain. So, despite a chronic shortage of supplies and equipment, Churchill agreed to send whatever he could spare to the Soviet Union. Clearly Stalin's demands for an immediate 'second front' or the intervention of British troops were both impractical. Instead, the government ordered the Admiralty to begin running regular supply convoys between Britain and the Soviet Union's Arctic ports of Archangel and Murmansk. So, the strategic lifeline of the Arctic convoys was created.

In August 1941 the first of these, a token convoy of just six merchant ships and a tanker, made the gruelling voyage to Archangel. This venture, codenamed Operation *Dervish*, was merely the first of many. Further outbound convoys would be given the prefix 'PQ', while returning ones became 'QP' convoys. Six of these convoys would reach Archangel or Murmansk before the end of the year, without loss. However, a brush between German destroyers and the minesweeper escort of PQ-6 suggested that the Germans were now aware of the new convoy route, and were preparing to contest the passage of any future convoys.

Sure enough, when PQ-7A attempted the voyage in late December, the merchantman *Waziristan* fell prey to *U-134*. The final outbound convoy

A German Type VIIc U-boat on the surface. During operations against the Arctic convoys, boats like this usually operated on the surface, despite the often appalling conditions. In winter, when near-perpetual darkness rendered air reconnaissance impractical, they alone were capable of detecting convoys in the region.

Armoured cruiser *Lützow* and heavy cruiser *Admiral Hipper*, viewed from the deck of a German destroyer during the Kriegsmarine's sortie against Convoy PQ-17 in July 1942. On that occasion *Lützow* ran aground, so she missed her chance to join the sortie.

Arctic convoy duties were tough on the crews of warships and merchant ships alike, but particularly so on crowded warships, where crews were often kept at their action stations for several hours at a time. Here, the crew of one of *Sheffield*'s turrets catch what sleep they can.

of the year, PQ-7B, reached Murmansk safely in early January, thanks to the poor weather which dogged her passage. Between September and December, four QP convoys made the return voyage from Archangel without loss, although the ships were badly battered by the brutal weather. This meant that before the end of the year, a total of 750 tanks, 800 fighter planes, 1,400 vehicles and 1 million tons of stores had reached the Soviet Union, to help keep it in the fight. It was clear though, that so far, the Allies had been lucky. Meanwhile, the Germans had been bolstering their strength in Norway, with more Luftwaffe squadrons, surface warships and U-boats. The next year, 1942, would see the Arctic campaign begin in earnest.

A factor was that Hitler now believed that the Allies planned to invade Norway. So, he ordered the battleship *Tirpitz* to be redeployed there, along with the battleship *Scharnhorst* and the cruisers *Admiral Scheer* and *Admiral Hipper*. This meant that by the spring, the Kriegsmarine would have a powerful enough naval presence in Norwegian waters to carry out surface attacks on the convoys. Meanwhile, the Kriegsmarine was making its presence felt in other ways. When Convoy PQ-8 reached the Barents Sea in early January 1942, it ran into a line of waiting U-boats. As a result, the destroyer *Matabele* was torpedoed and sunk, with the loss of all but two of her crew. A merchant ship was also damaged, but managed to limp on to Murmansk. For a while though, the destroyer was the only casualty. The next three convoys managed to reach Murmansk safely, as bad weather shielded them from the enemy.

The following convoy, PQ-13, was less fortunate. A clash between its escorts and German destroyers led to the destroyer *Z-26* being badly damaged. However, when the cruiser *Trinidad* tried to finish her off with a torpedo, the weapon malfunctioned, and having turned in a circle it struck the *Trinidad*. She managed to limp into Murmansk, but the *Z-26* sank with most of her crew still on board. Of the 19 merchant ships that made up the convoy, five of them never reached Murmansk. The next attempt in April was hampered by thick fog and dense pack ice. In the end, the bulk of Convoy PQ-14 returned to Iceland, falling in with the homeward-bound convoy QP-10 on the way. Only eight merchant ships continued on to Murmansk, and one of these fell prey to *U-403* on 16 April.

In general though, the Allied luck was holding, despite a marked increase in German activity. That year, of the five homeward-bound QP convoys between January and early April, only one merchantman was lost – a straggler from Convoy QP-8 overpowered by German destroyers. That convoy was particularly lucky, as the *Tirpitz* was out hunting for it, and the outward-bound convoy PQ-12. Thanks to rough weather, apart from that one straggler, the convoys were undetected, and the German battleship returned to Narvik. This German setback was reversed in mid-April, when Convoy QP-10 was detected and attacked. One merchantman was damaged and forced back to Murmansk, but two others were sunk by German bombers, and two more by *U-435*. By then, it was clear that the Germans had the wherewithal to seriously threaten this vital maritime supply line.

So, the next two outward-bound convoys, PQ-15 and PQ-16, both suffered losses – three merchantmen in the first convoy and seven in the second. These convoys had been notably larger than most of the earlier ones – PQ-16 consisted of 35 merchant ships. So, while in theory losses were still acceptable, to the merchant seamen who were subjected to five days of air attacks and the constant threat of being torpedoed, these voyages were hellish. When the last ships of PQ-16 reached Archangel it was 1 June, and so just a few weeks short of midsummer. The Admiralty were well aware that in the Arctic this meant near perpetual daylight, and so the chances of being detected by U-boats or search aircraft were extremely high. Once spotted, they would then be exposed to round-the-clock attack. Still, political pressure meant that the convoys would continue, however unsuitable the season might be.

The Altenfjord in the far north of Norway was an ideal forward base for the Kriegsmarine's Arctic battle group. It was sheltered from the elements, well protected from attack and lay within easy reach of the Arctic convoy route through the Barents Sea. Here, the battleship *Tirpitz* is seen at anchor there, her flak guns ready to repel any attack from the air.

On 27 June, the 35 merchantmen which made up Convoy PQ-17 left Reykjavik, accompanied by a powerful covering force, which for the first time included US Navy warships. Four days later, on 1 July, the convoy was detected by both a U-boat and a German reconnaissance plane to the north-east of Jan Mayen Island. The first air attack came the following afternoon, but then there was a reprieve until the convoy passed Bear Island. At the Admiralty, First Sea Lord Sir Dudley Pound became even more concerned when he learned that *Tirpitz* and *Admiral Hipper* were at sea. Presumably they would attempt to intercept the convoy. The Home Fleet's powerful Distant Covering Force was by then too far away to intervene. Fearing the worst, on the evening of 4 July Pound ordered the covering force of cruisers to withdraw to the west. Then, 40 minutes later, he ordered the convoy to scatter, and make for the Soviet ports.

One of the problems with winter operations beyond the Arctic Circle was the build-up of ice. Not only did it add to the top-hamper of a ship, making it more unstable in rough seas, but it also meant that weapons had to be continually freed of ice, a thankless task in such grim conditions.

German forward base in the Altenfjord, December 1942

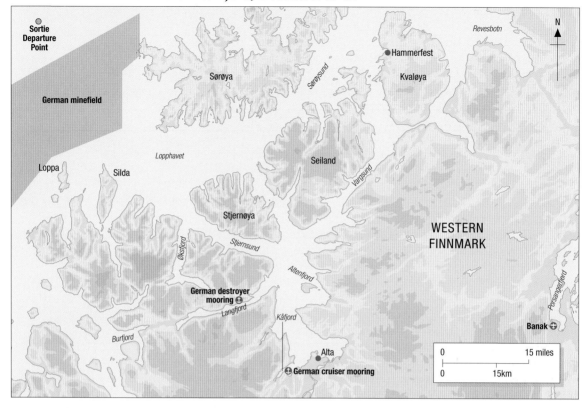

This, effectively, was the convoy's death knell. With American Rear Admiral Hamilton's covering force of cruisers and destroyers gone, the merchant ships were left to their own devices. To add a bitter irony to the tragedy that followed, *Tirpitz* and her consorts were recalled within hours of leaving the Altenfjord the following evening. In the Barents Sea though, the Luftwaffe and the U-boats had a field day. The small escort ships did what they could, gathering together some of their scattered charges, but otherwise the Germans were able to hunt down the Allied merchant ships with impunity. It was only as the surviving ships reached friendly ports that the full scale of the disaster became apparent. In all, 13 merchantmen were sunk by the Luftwaffe, and ten by U-boats. The total loss for the Germans was just six aircraft, shot down before the convoy scattered.

Sir Dudley Pound was heavily criticized for his decision, and with hindsight it might have been better to keep the convoy together, and rely on the naval commanders on the spot to decide what to do. However, the threat posed by *Tirpitz* was considerable. He also, probably, worried about the geopolitical ramifications if any of the four American warships in Hamilton's force were lost. What the disaster did do though, was deprive the Soviet army of hundreds of much-needed tanks, aircraft and trucks, which in turn led to increasing demands from Stalin that the Western Allies send more aid. Bowing to political pressure, Churchill agreed, despite sound advice from the Admiralty that sending another summer convoy to Murmansk was to risk another disaster.

On 2 September the 39 merchant ships that made up Convoy PQ-18 left Loch Ewe, bound for Iceland. One ship subsequently returned to Scotland with engine trouble. After dropping off three merchantmen and picking up eight more, the convoy continued on to Archangel. To avoid a repetition of the PQ-17 disaster, a sizeable portion of the Home Fleet was given the task of protecting the new convoy. A distant covering force of two battleships and a cruiser would take up position to the north-west of Jan Mayen Island, in case the *Tirpitz* made another sortie. This time the convoy escort included two small AA vessels, while a fighting escort of the light cruiser *Scylla* and 16 destroyers was there to protect the convoy during its passage through the Barents Sea. So too was the escort carrier *Avenger* and the two destroyers which accompanied her.

Three other forces would be involved. Two British groups, comprising five cruisers and a destroyer, were in the area, covering the homeward-bound QP-14, which was made up of the PQ-17 survivors and an expedition to Spitzbergen, to set up a refuelling station there. Finally there was an Anglo–Soviet local escort, there to guide the ships into port, made up of five Soviet destroyers and four British minesweepers. This was the most complex Arctic convoy operation yet, as the Allies fully expected they would have to fight the convoy through against heavy German opposition. In the end, the Germans failed to send a surface group to sea – the very factor that had tipped the balance against PQ-17. Thanks to Hitler's caution, it stayed at anchor. Instead the Germans attacked the convoy with ten U-boats and no fewer than 224 aircraft, 91 of which were torpedo bombers.

However, the first success went to the Allies, when *U-88* was sunk by three fighting-escort destroyers scouting ahead of the convoy. One of these was *Onslow*, which would take part in the battle of the Barents Sea three months later. Then, from 13 September on, the convoy was subjected to a succession of air and U-boat attacks, which lasted for nine gruelling days. In all, 13 merchant ships from the convoy were sunk, but the cost to the Germans had also been high. Three U-boats had been destroyed and 41 bombers shot down – losses they would be hard-pressed to replace. A total of 32 merchant ships made it safely into Archangel. It showed what could be achieved with thorough planning and grim determination.

This, however, would be the last outward-bound convoy of the season. Instead, a number of risky, independent passages were organized, as a gesture of support to the Soviets. These proved costly, and six ships were lost. There was also another homeward-bound convoy, which was partially protected by heavy gales. Even then, two of its merchant ships were torpedoed and sunk. So, there was a pause in the routine of convoys – a halt in activity while the Allies waited for the onset of the near perpetual darkness of the Arctic winter. Then it was hoped that the ships would stand a better chance of making it through the Barents Sea without being detected. The Allies knew full well that if the Germans spotted the next convoy, they'd do their utmost to destroy it.

An Allied convoy at sea. The merchant ships that made up these convoys were invariably arrayed in a grid pattern, with the ships deployed in columns, each made up of several ships. Each merchantman had its place in this formation, and the more vulnerable ships, usually the tankers, were commonly placed in the centre of the formation.

CHRONOLOGY

1941

22 June Commencement of Operation *Barbarossa* – Germany invades the Soviet Union.

12 August Operation *Dervish* – first Arctic convoy sails from Liverpool, bound for Archangel.

28 September The first homeward-bound convoy, QP-1, sails from Archangel, bound for Kirkwall.

29 September The first regular outward-bound convoy, PQ-1, sails from Hvalfjord in Iceland.

1942

5–9 March Operation *Sportpalast* – German sortie against convoys PQ-12 and PQ-8.

27 June Convoy PQ-17 sails from Reykjavik.

29 June *Jamaica* commissioned into Royal Navy.

2 July Operation *Rösselsprung* – German naval sortie against PQ-17.

4 July Order given for PQ-17 to scatter.

2 September Convoy PQ-18 sails from Loch Ewe.

October–November Operation *FB* – independent sailings to and from Soviet Union.

17 November Convoy QP-15 sails from Archangel.

15 December Convoy JW-51A sails from Loch Ewe.

22 December Convoy JW-51B sails from Loch Ewe.

24 December JW-51B first detected by German aircraft.

Force R refuels in Kola Inlet, after screening JW-51A.

25 December Western Escort detached from convoy JW-51B.

Fighting Escort joins JW-51B.

Oribi, *Vizalma* and five merchantmen lose contact with convoy due to bad weather.

Convoy JW-51A reaches Murmansk, without having been detected.

27 December Force R begins screening JW-51B.

29 December Accompanying destroyers detached from Force R.

Three merchantmen rejoin JW-51B, *Bramble* detached to locate others.

In winter, sea and weather conditions beyond the Arctic Circle were often extremely challenging. It meant that maintaining a visual lookout from the wildly pitching conning tower of a U-boat was often impossible. Instead, most U-boat commanders relied on their hydrophones to detect approaching convoys.

30 December	Convoy JW-51B detected by *U-354*.		briefly returns fire before withdrawing under cover of smoke screen.
	German battle group sails from the Altenfjord.	11.42	*Friedrich Eckoldt* engaged by Force R and left dead in the water.
	Convoy RA-51 sails from Murmansk.		*Lützow* opens fire on convoy, hitting the merchantman SS *Calobre*.

31 December 1942: battle of the Barents Sea

09.15	*Obdurate* sights three enemy destroyers.	11.45	British destroyers lay smoke to screen convoy.
09.30	*Friedrich Eckoldt*, *Richard Beitzen* and Z-29 open fire on *Obdurate*.	11.49	*Admiral Hipper* opens fire on British destroyers before they are hidden by snow squalls.
09.31–09.33	Sherwood leaves convoy to support *Obdurate*, accompanied by two more destroyers.	12.03	Burnett orders Force R to steam to the west, in pursuit of the Germans.
09.39	*Admiral Hipper* sighted by *Onslow*.	12.29–12.30	*Lützow* and *Sheffield* briefly exchange salvos.
09.40–09.41	*Achates* lays smoke to cover withdrawal of convoy, and attracts fire from *Admiral Hipper*.	12.33	Kummetz cancels the detachment of *Lützow* on an independent cruise.
09.44	British destroyers make dummy torpedo run at *Admiral Hipper*, which breaks contact.	12.34–12.35	Exchange of fire between Force R and *Admiral Hipper*. Burnett orders his ships to break visual contact.
10.08	Sherbrooke detaches *Obedient* to reinforce convoy escort.	12.40	Kummetz orders all his remaining ships to steam west, away from the convoy.
10.18	*Admiral Hipper* opens fire on *Onslow*, which is badly damaged and Sherbrooke is seriously wounded.	13.28 (approx.)	*Friedrich Eckoldt* blows up and sinks with all hands.
10.30	*Admiral Hipper* turns to the north-east, having lost contact with the British.	14.00	*Sheffield* loses radar contact with German ships. With contact broken, the battle ends.
10.36	*Admiral Hipper* sights and engages *Bramble*, which is badly damaged. The minesweeper sinks ten minutes later.	**1943**	
		1 January	*Vizalma* and a merchantman rejoin convoy.
10.40	Kummetz detaches *Friedrich Eckoldt* and *Richard Beitzen*.	3–4 January	JW-51B arrives in Murmansk.
11.15–11.18	*Achates* engaged by *Admiral Hipper*, and is badly damaged. She sinks two hours later.	5 January	Last straggler from JW-51B arrives in Murmansk.
11.30–11.34	Force R opens fire on *Admiral Hipper*, scoring three hits. The German cruiser	11 January	RA-51 arrives in Loch Ewe without being detected.

OPPOSING COMMANDERS

THE KRIEGSMARINE

The *Führer*, Adolf Hitler (1889–1945), never really understood seapower or the role of his navy. Setbacks such as the loss of *Graf Spee* and *Bismarck* made him reluctant to place his major warships in harm's way, and so he placed constraints on their operation, designed to reduce their exposure to risk.

Vizeadmiral (**Vice Admiral**) **Oskar Kummetz (1891–1980)**, who led the attack on Convoy JW-51B, was born near Neidenburg in East Prussia (now the Polish town of Nidzika), and was schooled locally. In 1910 he joined the Imperial German Navy as a cadet, and by 1913 he had become a *Leutnant-zur-See* (the equivalent of a senior midshipman in the Royal Navy). At the outbreak of World War I he was serving aboard the dreadnought *Helgoland*. The following year he was transferred to another dreadnought, the *Posen*. Then, in March 1916, he became an *Oberleutnant-zur-See* (sub-lieutenant), at which point he requested service in torpedo boats. The following month he had his wish, and as a watchkeeping officer he saw action at Jutland (May 1916). In March 1918 he was given command of the destroyer *G-10*. He remained in command of her until early 1919, by which time both he and his destroyer had become part of the new Reichsmarine.

Next he commanded a minehunter, which was used to help clear Germany's wartime minefields. Promotion to *Kapitänleutnant* (lieutenant) came in 1921, together with the command of another destroyer, *V-2*. In 1924, Kummetz became a staff officer, and three years later he commanded a destroyer half-division. He became a *Korvettenkapitän* (lieutenant commander) in 1928, and a *Fregattenkapitän* four years later, when he was given command of the Reichsmarine's small destroyer fleet. He finally reached the rank of *Kapitän-zur-See* (captain) in 1936, when he became the Chief of Staff to Admiral Boehm, who commanded the Kriegsmarine force, which was offering covert assistance to Franco's Nationalists during the Spanish Civil War. At the outbreak of World War II in September 1939, Kummetz was inspector of the Kriegsmarine's destroyer fleet.

In January 1940, he was promoted to *Konteradmiral* (rear admiral). During the invasion

FAR LEFT
Vizeadmiral Oskar Kummetz (1891–1980) drafted the plans for Operation *Regenbogen*, and implemented the attack perfectly. However, the sudden arrival of Force R took him by surprise, and given his incredibly restrictive rules of engagement, he was forced to call off the attack.

LEFT
Kapitän Hans Hartmann (1897–1976) was the flag captain of *Vizeadmiral* Kummetz, and so commanded the flagship *Admiral Hipper* during the battle. She was his first seagoing command of the war, having served in staff posts since 1939, but he handled her with commendable skill.

of Norway in April, he commanded the naval force which penetrated the Oslofjord. On 9 April, his flagship, the heavy cruiser *Blücher*, was sunk by the fire of Norwegian coastal batteries. Kummetz survived the disaster, and was awarded the Knight's Cross for his part in the capture of Oslo. In April 1942, he became a *Vizeadmiral*, and became *Befehlshaber der Krueuzer (BdK)*, the commander of cruisers, attached to *Gruppe Nord* (Group North), the Kriegsmarine battle group operating in Norwegian waters. He flew his flag in the heavy cruiser *Admiral Hipper*. He was served by a team of very competent staff officers, and together the admiral and his staff drew up the plans for what became Operation *Regenbogen*.

Konteradmiral Otto Klüber (1895–1953) controlled all Kriegsmarine forces in Norwegian waters, and from his floating headquarters at Narvik, he acted as a vital communications link between *Vizeadmiral* Kummetz and his superiors in Berlin and Kiel.

However, Kummetz was hindered by the operational restrictions imposed on him. In addition to the normal chain of command running between him and *Grossadmiral* Raeder, Hitler insisted on personally approving any operations in Arctic waters. His aim was to limit the risks his warships were exposed to, but it meant Kummetz was forced to fight a battle with undue caution. As a result, he was effectively prevented from fulfilling his mission, and pressing home his attack in the face of lighter opposition.

After the battle, Kummetz was censured by Hitler, but his Kriegsmarine superiors stood by him. So, the following March he was promoted to full *Admiral*, and given command of the newly created *Kamfgruppe der Kriegsmarine* (Naval Battle Group) based in Norway, which included the *Tirpitz* and *Scharnhorst*. Then, in September 1944, he became a *Generaladmiral*, and oversaw final operations in the Baltic until the end of the war.

Technically, despite holding a lower rank, his superior in terms of the chain of command was **Konteradmiral Otto Klüber (1895–1953)**, whose floating headquarters ship, the *Grille*, was moored off Narvik. A former chief of

staff to *Generaladmiral* Carls, he now coordinated all communications between Kummetz and his superiors in Kiel, and also the Luftwaffe commanders in Norway. In all operational matters though, Kummetz answered directly to Carls, and to Raeder. Kummetz's flag captain was *Kapitän-zur-See* Wilhelm Meisel (1891–1974), an experienced officer who had seen action during World War I, and who had commanded *Admiral Hipper* for over two years.

While Kummetz took direct control of the northern pincer of Operation *Regenbogen*, the southern pincer was directed by *Kapitän-zur-See* **Rudolf Stange (1899–1952)** of the *Lützow*. He was another experienced officer, and a specialist in aggressive destroyer tactics. Both Meisel and Stange would reach flag rank before the end of the war. This, like the promotion of Kummetz, stands as testimony to their professional competence. Unfortunately for them, all of these officers were constrained by the restrictions imposed on them by Hitler. Thanks to these, Kummetz and Stange were placed in a near impossible position during the operation. If Kummetz had been given greater freedom, the battle would almost certainly have taken a very different course.

Kapitän-zur-See Rudolf Stange (1899–1952) commanded *Lützow* during the battle. He'd joined the German navy during World War I, but the armoured cruiser was his first command. He was criticized for his undue caution while engaging the convoy, but this was due more to his orders than any lack of fighting spirit.

THE ROYAL NAVY

Rear Admiral Robert 'Bob' Burnett (1887–1959) was born in Aberdeenshire, but was sent to school in faraway Southsea, and joined the navy when he was 16. When war broke out in 1914, he was a lieutenant in charge of physical training, but was soon transferred to a destroyer attached to the Grand Fleet. He ended the war as a lieutenant commander, and returned to fitness instruction. However, in 1923, as a commander, he was given the command of a sloop. In 1931, after a spell as the first lieutenant on the battleship *Rodney*, he became a captain, and was given command of a destroyer flotilla based in the Far East. Various shore-based appointments followed, but in 1940 he was given an acting flag rank, and became the naval aide to King George VI. His promotion to rear admiral was confirmed in January 1941. In the spring of 1942, after a spell commanding the navy's minesweepers, he was given control of the Home Fleet's destroyers. This gave him crucial insight into the whole Arctic convoy operation.

So, when the convoys resumed, Burnett was given temporary command of the cruisers protecting the two JW-51 convoys, and temporarily flew his flag in the light cruiser *Sheffield*. Burnett used to joke, slapping his bottom and telling people that's where his brains were. He also described himself as a 'clubswinger' admiral, the naval term for a physical training instructor. In fact, Bob Burnett had an instinctive grasp of naval tactics, and proved himself to be a superbly gifted commander. During the action in defence of Convoy JW-51B, Burnett demonstrated his ability to think on his feet and to read a battle. When faced with the threat posed by *Admiral Hipper*, he

Rear Admiral Robert 'Bob' Burnett, on the bridge of the destroyer *Faulknor*, flotilla leader of the F-class destroyers, speaking to her commander, Captain Scott-Moncrieff (right). Burnett's instinctive grasp of naval tactics helped ensure the convoy was saved, and the German battle group driven off.

reacted with speed, decisiveness and aggression. He also exuded a confidence in action that his men found reassuring, and this helped to underpin the deep affection his sailors had for him.

He was, in other words, the epitome of the 'fighting admiral', whose abilities were based on sound leadership and his own instincts as much as more tangible factors such as relative strength and firepower. As a result, he succeeded effectively in driving off a more powerful opponent by using highly aggressive tactics, and so gaining a marked psychological advantage over his more cautious opponent. He was rewarded with a knighthood, and eventually by promotion to the rank of vice admiral. Even more impressively, if his performance at the Barents Sea wasn't enough, a year later he pulled off a similar feat, harassing the German battleship *Scharnhorst* off North Cape, and driving her into the guns of the battleship *Duke of York*. Still, Burnett wouldn't have been able to defend Convoy JW-51B if it hadn't been for the equally decisive actions of another quick-thinking commander – Captain Sherbrooke.

Captain Robert Sherbrooke (1901–72) the newly appointed captain (D), commanding the 17th Destroyer Flotilla was in charge of the convoy's fighting escort during the battle. The aggressive tactics he used to fend off the German attack earned him a Victoria Cross, and a near-fatal injury.

Captain Robert Sherbrooke (1901–72) was born into a naval family, and brought up in Oxton Hall near Newark in Nottinghamshire. He was schooled in Osborne on the Isle of Wight, and joined the Navy as a midshipman in 1917. He served out the war on the dreadnought *Canada*, and spent the next 15 years serving on a variety of battleships and destroyers. In 1936, as a newly promoted commander, Sherbrooke was given command of a destroyer, based in Gibraltar. He clearly had an aptitude for destroyer service, as apart from a pre-war staff course, he remained a destroyer captain until the injuries he suffered in the Barents Sea forced him ashore. He won the DSO in 1940, while commanding the destroyer *Cossack* at the second battle of Narvik. He then spent a year leading a destroyer group based in Freetown, Sierra Leone, before his promotion to captain in June 1942. He was duly given command of the 17th Destroyer Flotilla, which formed part of the Home Fleet. He took up his position as the flotilla's captain (Destroyers) in late November, just weeks before the battle.

His predecessor had been well liked, and after Sherbrooke hoisted his command pennant in the destroyer *Onslow*, his men found him reserved and taciturn. However, they would soon discover their new captain (D) was a fighting captain in the mould of the much more likeable Bob Burnett. By then, his small staff was experienced in the business of protecting Arctic convoys, and Sherbrooke found his ships were well run and fully ready for action. When the time for action came, on 30 December, Sherbrooke proved himself a truly gifted commander. His quick thinking when he sighted German destroyers approaching the convoy played a large part in protecting his charges, and the aggression he showed in tackling his more powerful opponents was key to stealing the initiative of the battle from Kummetz. He was deservedly awarded the Victoria Cross for his actions. Sherbrooke was badly wounded during the battle, and this effectively put paid to his wartime seagoing career. After a string of shore postings, he finally returned to sea as a cruiser captain in 1945. He finally retired from the service with the rank of rear admiral.

During the battle, Rear Admiral Burnett, as the senior officer in the area, was in command of all forces in the battle area. However, until Burnett's dramatic intervention in the fight, Captain Sherbrooke was in command of the convoy's defence. He also assumed tactical control over both the convoy itself, through its commodore, and its close escort of corvettes, trawlers and a minesweeper. Both of these British officers still answered to **Admiral Sir John Tovey (1885–1971)**, the commander-in-chief of the Home Fleet. Tovey was a cerebral commander, and a thoroughgoing professional, and so he realized that his duty was to command rather than to lead.

So, when the Arctic convoys resumed that December, he controlled their movements and defence from his flagship *King George V*, moored in Scapa Flow. He left it to his deputy, Vice Admiral Fraser, to lead the distant covering force, as communications at sea were less secure. Tovey was also well aware that his commanders on the spot – Burnett and Sherbrooke – would have to defend the convoy as best they could, without referring every decision back to him. Only they could know the full tactical circumstances. As a result, these two British commanders were given the leeway they needed to fight, in sharp contrast to their German counterpart.

As the commander of the British Home Fleet, Admiral John Tovey had the task of protecting the Arctic convoys, and ensuring his ships were able to counter any German sortie. Despite his detailed plans for the resumption of convoy operations that December, JW-51B was still left vulnerable to attack.

OPPOSING FORCES

THE KRIEGSMARINE

The strength of the Kriegsmarine's force in Norway had reached its operational peak the previous summer, when it sallied out to attack Convoy PQ-17. The fleet had suffered a number of setbacks, which considerably reduced its pool of available warships. While *Tirpitz* was in the Trondheimfjord, and therefore theoretically able to join any sortie, the battleship was undergoing a much-needed programme of self-maintenance, which meant her crew were doing these vital repairs themselves. So, her operational readiness had been reduced, and she would remain out of active service for the remainder of the winter. *Scharnhorst* had been undergoing repairs in Kiel until October, but had still not been redeployed to Norway. Her sister ship, *Gneisenau*, was in Gotenhaven, and so badly damaged that she had been decommissioned.

The armoured cruiser *Admiral Scheer* had returned to Kiel for a refit, as had the heavy cruiser *Prinz Eugen*, which was due to return to Norway in the New Year, in company with the *Scharnhorst*. Of the fleet's light cruisers, *Emden* and *Leipzig* were in home waters, being used as training ships. The *Köln* was in the Arctic, where she had recently been joined by the *Nürnberg*. These though, were considered too vulnerable to take part in any offensive operation. So, of all these battleships and cruisers, apart from the *Köln*, only the armoured cruiser *Lützow* and the heavy cruiser *Admiral Hipper* were fully operational that December, in Norwegian waters, and ready for operations against the Arctic convoys.

LÜTZOW

Deutschland-class armoured cruiser

Displacement:	16,200 tons (fully laden)		
Commissioned:	1933		
Length overall:	610ft 3in.		
Beam:	70ft 10in.	Protection:	2¼–2½in. belt, 1½in. deck, 3¼–5½in. turrets, 6in. conning tower
Draught:	24ft 3in.		
Propulsion:	Two shafts, eight MAN diesel engines, producing 54,000shp	Radar:	FUMo22 (surface search), FuMo26 (surface fire control)
Maximum speed:	28 knots	Aircraft:	One catapult and up to two aircraft (Arado A196 float planes)
Armament:	Six 28cm SKC/28 guns in two triple turrets, eight 15cm SKC/28 guns in single turrets, six 10.5cm SKC/30 AA guns in three twin mounts, eight 3.7cm AA guns in four twin mounts, 18 20mm AA guns (ten in single and two in quadruple mounts), eight 53.3cm G7a torpedoes in two quadruple launchers	Complement:	1,150 men

The armoured cruiser *Lützow*, in the Bogenfjord near Narvik during the late summer of 1942. As in the Altenfjord, German capital ships at anchor were protected by a screen of anti-torpedo nets, and guarded by anti-submarine vessels and destroyers.

The *Lützow*, formerly the *Deutschland*, was a *panzerschiffe* – what the British described as a pocket battleship, because of her powerful armament of six 28cm guns in two triple turrets. Her armour though, was more akin to that of a cruiser. She and her sister ships, *Admiral Scheer* and *Admiral Graf Spee*, had been primarily designed as commerce raiders. With their diesel propulsion systems and extensive range, they were well suited to this role, but the loss of *Bismarck* in May 1941 brought the Kriegsmarine campaign of surface commerce raiding to an end. Instead, the *panzerschiffe*, now redesignated as armoured cruisers, were used to bolster the surface fleet. With their powerful armament, they were useful warships, and if *Admiral Scheer* could only get within range of an unprotected convoy, then her guns could wreak havoc.

Admiral Hipper was a more conventional heavy cruiser. Her eight 20.3cm guns made her the equivalent of the County-class heavy cruisers of the Royal Navy, although she was a much better-designed ship, and marginally better protected too. She too would be devastatingly effective if she managed to intercept an Allied convoy successfully. Her crew had trained to operate their optical rangefinders and radar in the poor light conditions they expected to

ADMIRAL HIPPER

Admiral Hipper-class heavy cruiser

Displacement:	18,200 tons (fully laden)
Commissioned:	1939
Length overall:	665ft 8in.
Beam:	69ft 10½in.
Draught:	25ft 11in.
Propulsion:	Three shafts, three Blohm & Voss turbines, 12 La Mont boilers, generating 132,000shp
Maximum speed:	32½ knots
Armament:	Eight 20.3cm SKC/34 guns in four twin turrets, 12 10.5cm SKC/33 guns in six twin mounts, 12 37mm AA guns in six twin mounts, 18 20mm flak guns in single mounts, 12 53.3cm G7a torpedoes in four triple launchers, with 12 reloads
Protection:	1½–3¼in. belt, ½–1¼in. deck, 2¼–6¼in. turrets, 2–6in. conning tower
Radar:	FuMo26 (surface fire control)
Aircraft:	One catapult and up to three aircraft (Arado A196 float planes)
Complement:	1,600 men

The German heavy cruiser *Admiral Hipper* in dry dock. The sister ship of the more famous *Prinz Eugen*, *Hipper* served much of her wartime career in Norwegian waters, where her very presence served as a threat to the Arctic convoys.

find in the Barents Sea that December, and Kummetz was sure the cruiser – his flagship – would make a good account of herself. His problem, however, was that the two cruisers weren't enough. In order to locate the convoy, he needed more warships to extend his search radius and to protect the cruisers from lighter enemy warships.

Fortunately for *Konteradmiral* Kummetz, the two cruisers were ably supported by a powerful force of six destroyers. Three of these were Z-1- or Maas-class destroyers: *Richard Beitzen* (*Z-4*) was a Type 34 destroyer, while her almost identical sisters, *Theodor Riedel* (*Z-6*) and *Friedrich Eckoldt* (*Z-16*), were Type 34A vessels. These were the first true destroyers to be built for the navy after World War I, having been designed without any consideration of the restrictions placed on Germany by the Versailles Treaty. They were fast, sleek and well armed, carrying five single 12.7cm guns and eight torpedoes in two quadruple launchers. Ship for ship, they were larger and more robust than their British counterparts. They also had their faults. They were prone to engine malfunctions, and their forecastles had to be raised to reduce their tendency to ship water over the bows.

The German heavy cruiser *Admiral Hipper*, pictured in Norwegian waters during late 1942. Under the skilful command of *Kapitän* Hartmann she performed her duties admirably, drawing off the convoy's destroyer escort. All went well until she was ambushed in turn by Force R.

RICHARD BEITZEN (Z-4), THEODOR RIEDEL (Z-6), FRIEDRICH ECKOLDT (Z-16)

Type 1934-class (*Z-4*) and 1934A-class (*Z-6, Z-16*) destroyers

Displacement:	3,156–3,165 tons (fully laden)
Commissioned:	1937–38
Length overall:	Type 34: 391ft 5in., Type 34A: 397ft
Beam:	37ft
Draught:	13ft 1in.
Propulsion:	Two shafts, two Wagner turbines, six Wagner boilers, generating 70,000shp (*Z-16* fitted with Benson turbines and boilers, with identical performance)
Maximum speed:	38 knots
Armament:	Five 12.7cm SKC/34 guns in single mounts, four 37mm flak guns in two twin mounts, four 20mm flak guns in single mounts, eight 53.3cm G7a torpedoes in two quadruple launchers
Radar:	FuMo21 (surface search)
Complement:	315 men

German Type 36A destroyers in the Altenfjord. Due to their relatively poor seakeeping qualities, these ships were ill suited to operations in the rough waters of the Arctic. However, *Vizeadmiral* Kummetz needed them to help locate the Allied convoy.

Of the remaining three available destroyers, *Z-29* and *Z-30* were Type 36A-class vessels, which were slightly larger than the others, and *Z-31*, which was virtually identical, but formed part of the Type 36A (Mob) class. Collectively, as part of the 8th (Narvik) Destroyer Flotilla, they were often described as Z-23- or Narvik-class destroyers. They were armed similarly to the earlier destroyers, but with larger 15cm guns. It was decided to replace their two single forward guns with one twin turret, but this modification was problematic, and apart from *Z-31*, these destroyers didn't receive the twin turret before Operation *Regenbogen* began. *Z-31* also carried an extra single 15cm gun, mounted on her stern superstructure. Like their predecessors, these destroyers were larger than their British opponents, and their powerful armament gave them a considerable edge in gunnery.

In any other season, a sortie by German surface ships would have enjoyed support from both the Luftwaffe and U-boats. However, that November the Allies had invaded North Africa, so consequently the bulk of the Luftwaffe bombers which had been deployed in northern Norway had been sent to the Mediterranean. So, the air attacks levelled at PQ-17 and PQ-18 represented a

Z-29, Z-30, Z-31

Type 1936A (*Z-29, Z-30*) and 1936A (Mob) class (*Z-31*) destroyers

Displacement:	3,597 tons (fully laden)
Commissioned:	1941–42
Length overall:	416ft 5in.
Beam:	39ft 4in.
Draught:	13ft 1in.–15ft 2in.
Propulsion:	Two shafts, two Wagner turbines, six Wagner boilers, generating 70,000shp
Maximum speed:	38½ knots
Armament:	*Z-29, Z-30*: four 15cm SKC/36 guns in single mounts, four 37mm flak guns in two twin mounts, 13 20mm flak guns in two quad and five single mounts, eight 53.3cm G7a torpedoes in two quadruple launchers; *Z-31*: five 15cm SKC/36 guns in one twin and three single mounts, four 37mm flak guns in two twin mounts, nine 20mm flak guns in one quad and five single mounts, eight 53.3cm G7a torpedoes in two quadruple launchers
Radar:	FuMo21 (surface search)
Complement:	321 men

The German Type 36A destroyer *Z-30* at anchor in a Norwegian fjord during 1942–43. She formed part of the southern pincer of the German battle group, and briefly saw action during the closing stages of the engagement.

high water mark in terms of Luftwaffe activity in the Arctic. Besides, in the Arctic winter there was nothing for the bombers to do. While reconnaissance flights were still sent up, and they patrolled far to the west of the Barents Sea, the short window of daylight meant that they would be hard-pressed to locate a convoy. As for air attacks, that same lack of daylight made bombing operations all but impossible.

So, the only effective reconnaissance tool available to the Kriegsmarine that winter was its small screen of U-boats. The 11th Flotilla based in Narvik was responsible for patrolling the approaches to the Barents Sea that winter, and consequently five U-boats were deployed across the likely path of an outward-bound convoy. It was one of these, *U-354*, that first spotted Convoy JW-51A, and put Operation *Regenbogen* into action. Still, the U-boats weren't really there to carry out attacks, unless a suitable target presented itself. Instead, their job was to spot the convoy and then shadow it if possible, passing on sighting reports that would then allow German surface ships to intercept it. So, in essence, that December, if the next outward-bound convoy was to be attacked, the task fell to Admiral Kummetz and his small force of cruisers and destroyers.

THE ROYAL NAVY

For the Allies, this whole operation centred around the 45 merchant ships of the three Arctic convoys which would pass through the Barents Sea that December. Two of the convoys, JW-51A and JW-51B, were outward bound, sailing from Loch Ewe in Scotland to the Soviet port of Murmansk. Of these, JW-51A consisted of 16 merchantmen and JW-51B another 15 of them. The homeward-bound convoy RA-51, made up of 14 merchant ships, was the last of the three to sail, and would be making the reverse journey, from Murmansk to Loch Ewe. Each convoy was protected by its own convoy escort, most of which was supplied by Western Approaches command. In the case of JW-51B, this escort was divided into two groups. One would escort the convoy as far as Iceland, while the second would accompany it to Murmansk.

The larger escorts were provided by the Home Fleet. For JW-51B, these were divided into three groups. The fighting escort of six destroyers would accompany the convoy on its voyage from Iceland to the Soviet Union, while a covering force of two light cruisers, *Sheffield* and *Jamaica*, would screen the passage of all three convoys. This group, designated Force R, was commanded by Rear Admiral Burnett. In addition, there was a distant covering force, which shadowed the two outbound convoys until they reached a point between Jan Mayen Island and Bear Island. For JW-51A, this was made up of the battleship *King George V*, the heavy cruiser *Berwick* and three destroyers. Convoy JW-51B was covered by the battleship *Anson*, the heavy cruiser *Cumberland* and five destroyers.

RA-51 was accompanied by a small close escort of a minesweeper and four trawlers, and a fighting escort of six destroyers. Its distant covering force was made up of two battleships, *King George V* and *Howe*, the light cruiser *Bermuda* and six destroyers. In addition, a screen of British submarines was stationed off the entrance to the Altenfjord, to raise the alarm if the German surface fleet made a sortie. This immensely complicated operation was coordinated by Admiral Tovey on board his flagship, *King George V*.

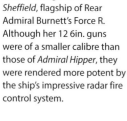

The British light cruiser *Sheffield*, flagship of Rear Admiral Burnett's Force R. Although her 12 6in. guns were of a smaller calibre than those of *Admiral Hipper*, they were rendered more potent by the ship's impressive radar fire control system.

For the purposes of the account of the battle, we need only concern ourselves with the ships that participated in the battle of 31 December. The two light cruisers of Burnett's Force R were similar in terms of both general appearance and fighting potential. *Sheffield* was a Southampton-class light cruiser, armed with 12 6in. guns in four turrets, and six 21in. torpedoes in three triple launchers. *Jamaica* was a Fiji (or Colony) class cruiser, with a similar armament. She was slightly smaller than *Sheffield*, and displaced less. Both ships lacked much in the way of protection, but their belt was still comparable with the two larger German cruisers. Where they had an edge was in the efficiency of their radar, and in the speed at which their salvos could be delivered.

As for Captain Sherbrooke's fighting escort of destroyers, all but one were O-class vessels, most of which had entered service that year. Their designed armament of four 4.7in. guns in four single mountings and eight 21in. torpedoes in four quadruple mounts was fairly standard for British war-built destroyers, but their efficiency was enhanced by their radar, which permitted a limited degree of radar-controlled gunnery. However, three of his destroyers mounted older 4in. guns due to a shortage of the larger weapons. *Orwell*, as flotilla leader, also carried an additional 4in. gun in lieu of her after torpedo tubes.

The last of Sherbrooke's destroyers was the *Achates*, an 'A class' which first entered service over 12 years before. She was slightly smaller than the other destroyers, lacked their more modern fire control systems, and

The King George V-class battleship *Anson*, flagship of Vice Admiral Fraser, second-in-command of the Home Fleet. As the main unit of the Distant Covering Force, her primary job was to counter any sortie by the *Tirpitz* or other German capital ships which might venture from either Trondheim or Narvik.

JAMAICA

Fiji-class light cruiser

Displacement:	10,450 tons (fully laden)		
Commissioned:	1942		
Length overall:	555ft 6in.		
Beam:	62ft	Protection:	3¼–3½in. belt, 2in. deck, 2in. turrets
Draught:	19ft 10in.	Radar:	Type 27 (air warning), Type 273 (surface search), Type 284, Type 285 (both surface fire control)
Propulsion:	Four shafts, four Parsons turbines, four Admiralty boilers, generating 72,500shp		
Maximum speed:	31½ knots		
Armament:	12 6in. Mk. XXIII guns in four triple mounts, eight 4in. QF Mk. XVI high-angle guns	Aircraft:	One catapult and two aircraft (Supermarine Walrus float planes)
	in four double mounts, two quadruple 2pdr pom-poms, two quad .5in. machine guns, six 21in. Mk. IX torpedoes in two triple mounts	Complement:	733 men

The Kenya-class or colony-class light cruiser *Jamaica*, part of Force R, was similar to the *Sheffield*, but was slightly smaller and more compact. However, she did have a similar suite of radar and fire control equipment, and her guns were every bit as deadly as those of Burnett's flagship.

mounted a reduced main armament and suite of torpedoes, to compensate for her additional anti-submarine capability. So, Sherbrooke took account for this in his defensive plan. While *Achates* would screen the convoy, the O-class destroyers would aggressively fight off any enemy attack.

As for the close escort of minesweepers, corvettes and trawlers, none of these ships were any match for a German destroyer, let alone one of the cruisers. The Halcyon-class minesweeper *Bramble* carried two single 4in. guns, with no modern fire control system, while the two Flower-class corvettes and two armed trawlers carried a single 4in. gun apiece. Their sole purpose was to screen the convoy from U-boats, and to act as rescue ships if any ship was sunk. During the battle, only *Bramble* was forced into a gunnery exchange, and this one-sided duel ended with her sinking. So, until Force R could appear, it was up to Sherbrooke's destroyers to keep the enemy at bay.

ACHATES

A-class destroyer

Displacement:	1,773 tons (fully laden)	Maximum speed:	35 knots
Commissioned:	1930	Armament:	Two 4.7in. QF Mk. IX, low-angle guns in single mounts, one 3in. QF AA gun in single mount, one Hedgehog depth charge launcher, two single 2pdr pom-poms, two single 20mm Oerlikons, four 21in. Mk. IX torpedoes in a quadruple mount
Length overall:	323ft		
Beam:	32ft 3in.		
Draught:	12ft 3in.		
Propulsion:	Two shafts, two Brown-Curtiss turbines, three Admiralty boilers, producing 34,000shp	Radar:	Type 271 (surface search)
		Complement:	138 men

ONSLOW, OBDURATE, ORWELL, OBEDIENT

O-class destroyers

Displacement:	2,365 tons (fully laden)		IX high-angle guns, one 4in. QF Mk. II high-angle gun), one quadruple 2pdr pom-pom, four single 20mm Oerlikons, eight 21in. Mk. IX torpedoes in two quadruple mounts (one mount in *Onslow*)
Commissioned:	1941–42		
Length overall:	345ft		
Beam:	35ft		
Draught:	13ft 6in.	Radar:	Type 286 (surface search/air warning), Type 291 (surface search/ air warning)
Propulsion:	Two shafts, two Parsons turbines, two Admiralty boilers, generating 40,000shp		
Maximum speed:	37 knots	Complement:	217 men
Armament:	Three 4in. QF Mk. V high-angle guns in single mounts (*Onslow*: Four 4.7in. QF Mk.		

ORDERS OF BATTLE

KRIEGSMARINE

GERMAN BATTLE GROUP, OPERATION *REGENBOGEN*

Vizeadmiral Kummetz
Northern Force (*Vizeadmiral* Kummetz)
Admiral Hipper (Admiral Hipper-class heavy cruiser) (*Kapitän* Hartmann)
Flagship, *Vizeadmiral* Kummetz
Richard Beitzen (*Z-4*) (Type 1934-class destroyer) (*Fregattenkapitän* von Davidson)
Friedrich Eckoldt (*Z-16*) (Type 1934A-class destroyer) (*Kapitänleutnant* Bachmann)
Flagship of *Kapitän* Schemmel, commanding 5th Destroyer Flotilla
Z-29 (Type 1936A-class destroyer) (*Korvettenkapitän* Rechel)
Southern Force (*Kapitän* Stange)
Lützow (Deutschland-class armoured cruiser) (*Kapitän* Stange)
Theodor Riedel (*Z-6*) (Type 1934A-class destroyer) (*Korvettenkapitän* Reide)
Z-30 (Type 1936A-class destroyer) (*Fregattenkapitän* Kaiser)
Z-31 (Type 1936A) (Mob) class destroyer (*Korvettenkapitän* Alberts)

ROYAL NAVY

Note: in the lists below, ships indicated with an asterix were not present at the battle.

FORCE R

(Rear Admiral Burnett)
Sheffield (Southampton-class light cruiser) (Captain Clarke)
Flagship, Rear Admiral Burnett
Jamaica (Fiji-class light cruiser) (Captain Storey)
Detached on 29 December
Opportune (O-class destroyer) (Commander Lee-Barber)
Matchless (M-class destroyer) (Lieutenant Commander Mowlam)

FIGHTING ESCORT

(Captain Sherbrooke)
Achate (A-class destroyer) (Lieutenant Commander Johns)
Bulldog (B-class destroyer) (Lieutenant Commander Lee)*
Onslow (O-class destroyer) (Captain Sherbrooke)
Orwell (O-class destroyer) (Lieutenant Commander Austen)
Obdurate (O-class destroyer) (Lieutenant Commander Sclater)
Obedient (O-class destroyer) (Lieutenant Commander Kinloch)
Oribi (O-class destroyer) (Lieutenant Commander McBeath)*

CLOSE ESCORT

(Commander Rust)
Bramble (Halcyon-class minesweeper) (Commander Rust)
Rhododendron (Flower-class corvette) (Lieutenant Sayers RNR)
Hyderabad (Flower-class corvette) (Lieutenant Hickman RNR)
Vizalma (ASW trawler) (Acting Lieutenant Anglebeck RNR)*
Northern Gem (ASW trawler) (Skipper Lieutenant Mullender RNR)

WESTERN ESCORT

(Lieutenant Commander Powlett)
Blankney (Hunt-class escort destroyer) (Lieutenant Commander Powlett)*
Chiddingfold (Hunt-class escort destroyer) (Lieutenant Argles)*
Ledbury (Hunt-class escort destroyer) (Lieutenant Commander Hill)*

DISTANT ESCORT

(Vice Admiral Fraser)
Anson (King George V-class battleship) (Captain Kinahan)*
Flagship, Vice Admiral Fraser (not present at battle)
Cumberland (Kent-class heavy cruiser) (Captain Maxwell-Hyslop)*
Forester (F-class destroyer) (Lieutenant Commander Burnett)*
Icarus (I-class destroyer) (Lieutenant Commander Walmsley)*
Impulsive (I-class destroyer) (Lieutenant Commander Roper)*

SUBMARINE SCREEN

(off Altenfjord)
HrMS[1] *0-14* (Dutch O-12 class submarine) (Lieutenant Commander Goosens RNN)*
Graph (*P-715*) (former German Type-VIIC U-boat *U-570*) (Lieutenant Marriott)*
Seadog (*P-216*) (S-class submarine) (Lieutenant Martin)*
Trespasser (*P-312*) (T-class submarine) (Lieutenant Favell)*
Unruly (*P-49*) (U-class submarine) (Lieutenant Fyfe)*

DETACHED SERVICE

(Kola Inlet)
Seagull (Halcyon-class minesweeper) (Lieutenant Commander Pollock)*

CONVOY JW-51B

Ship	Nationality	Tonnage	Year built	Cargo
Ballot	Panamanian	6,131	1922	vehicles, tanks, aircraft
Calobre	Panamanian	6,891	1919	vehicles, tanks, fuel
Daldorch	British	5,571	1930	vehicles
Dover Hill†	British	5,818	1918	vehicles, tanks, aircraft, fuel
*Empire Archer**	British	7,031	1942	vehicles, tanks, aircraft
Empire Emerald	British	8,032	1941	fuel
Executive	American	4,978	1920	vehicles, aircraft, fuel
Jefferson Meyers	American	7,582	1920	vehicles, aircraft, fuel
JH La Trobe	American	7,191	1942	vehicles, tanks, aircraft
Pontfield	British	8,319	1939	fuel
Puerto Rican	American	6,076	1919	vehicles, tanks, aircraft
RW Emerson	American	7,176	1942	vehicles, tanks, aircraft, fuel
Vermont	British	5,670	1919	vehicles, aircraft, fuel
Yorkmar	British	5,612	1919	vehicles, fuel

† *Dover Hill* was forced to return to Iceland with weather-related boiler damage.

* *Empire Archer* was the flagship of Convoy Commodore Captain Melhuish RIN.

1 HrMS stands for *Harer Majesteits* (Her Majesty's) Ship – part of the Royal Netherlands Navy.

OPPOSING PLANS

THE KRIEGSMARINE

By late 1942, it was clear that the Allies would try to resume their Arctic convoy sailings under cover of the dark Arctic winter. Given the near-permanent darkness at that time of year, with just a few hours of twilight around noon, Luftwaffe reconnaissance aircraft, while actively patrolling, would find it nearly impossible to locate an approaching convoy. So, it was up to the Kriegsmarine's thin U-boat screen to provide *Vizeadmiral* Kummetz with the advance warning he required to plan a sortie. The problem here was that given the often atrocious weather conditions in the region, the sighting of a convoy from a U-boat couldn't be guaranteed, either by using hydrophones or lookouts. This, together with less reliable radio-direction finding and intelligence gathering sources, were all the tools Kummetz had at his disposal.

So, from September on, plans were developed which could be implemented as soon as another outward-bound convoy was detected. This plan was approved by *Grossadmiral* Raeder in Berlin, having done the rounds of

The forward guns of German heavy cruiser *Admiral Hipper*. These 20.3cm SKC/34 guns had a range far in excess of the visibility available in the Arctic, and so, to make the most of his guns, *Vizeadmiral* Kummetz decided to attack the convoy during the brief period of twilight before noon.

Operation *Regenbogen*: the German sortie

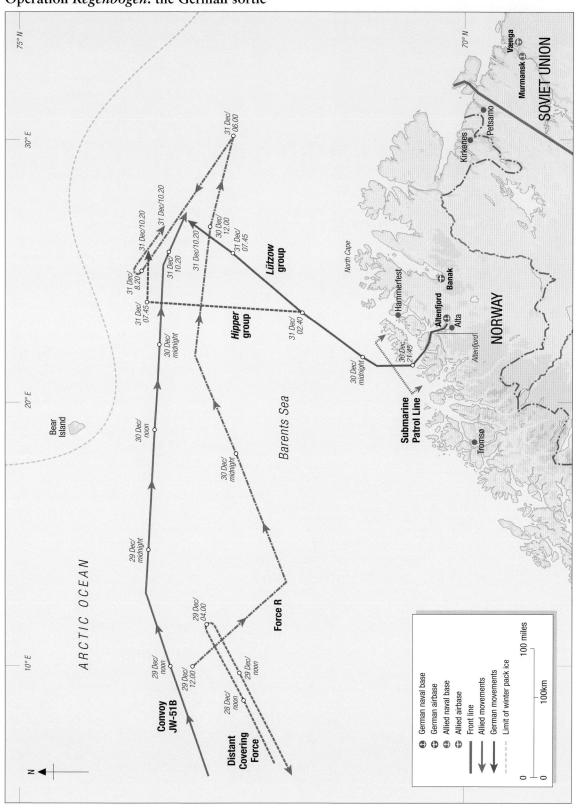

One of the key advantages enjoyed by the Allies during the naval war was their access to German naval signals, following the British capture of an Enigma coding machine, and the decryption of German cyphers. Thanks to the codebreakers, the Home Fleet's commander was aware that the Kreigsmarine's battle group in the Altenfjord was preparing to attack the December convoys.

the various relevant naval headquarters, but ultimately it was accepted that it would be Kummetz, as the *Befehlshaber der Kreuzer* (*BdK*) based in northern Norway, who would put it into action. By early December, this plan even had a name, Operation *Regenbogen*. Given the lack of other suitable surface warships, it centred around an attack on the convoy by Kummetz's powerful battle group – the heavy cruiser *Admiral Hipper*, the armoured cruiser *Lützow*, and the six destroyers currently available to him in the Altenfjord. The operational plan was flexible enough to be altered according to circumstances, but at its heart was a very simple premise.

It was expected that while an outward-bound convoy would be protected by more powerful units of the Home Fleet, including battleships, aircraft carriers and heavy cruisers, from previous operations it was considered likely that these wouldn't venture as far east as the Barents Sea. Instead, the convoy would be protected by relatively light forces – corvettes, minesweepers and armed trawlers, there to protect it from U-boat attacks, and by a more powerful escort of about six destroyers. If larger warships ventured that far east, then it was thought likely these would most probably be light cruisers, and these would be expected to maintain a distance from the convoy, to avoid attracting the attention of any U-boats which were shadowing the merchant ships. In other words, the convoy would be relatively lightly protected. If the bulk of these escorts could be drawn away, the convoy itself would be at the mercy of the attacker.

The presumption was that any outward-bound convoy would be sailing on an easterly base course, and making roughly 8 knots. While the convoy might zig-zag to deter U-boat attacks, it would still stick to this base course and speed. Once the convoy was located, and ideally shadowed as well, the German battle group would put to sea from the Altenfjord under cover of darkness, and reach a position astern of the convoy the following morning. By attacking from the west, it would give Kummetz a slight edge in terms of visibility, as his opponents would be silhouetted by what little light there was. It would divide into two groups, each consisting of a cruiser and half of the available destroyers. Effectively, these would form two pincers. While one pincer would circle to the north of the convoy, the other would do the same to the south.

Then, ideally at around 09.00, when the Arctic darkness gave way to a noon twilight, the northern pincer would make its move, closing with the convoy from the north, until visual contact was made. At that point, it was expected that the escorting destroyers would form up to protect the convoy from this threat, placing themselves between the Germans and the convoy. The convoy was also expected to alter course towards the south or south-east, away from the Germans. Whatever escort remained with it was going to be very light indeed – probably no more than the close escort, and therefore no match for a destroyer, let alone a cruiser. By altering course, the convoy and its weak escorts would now be heading directly towards the southern arm of the pincer.

Effectively, the northern pincer would be the hammer, drawing off the escorting destroyers, and driving the convoy towards the southern group – the anvil. Kummetz knew that in those poor light conditions his northern pincer would be particularly vulnerable to torpedo attack. So, to avoid unnecessary risk, its ships would keep at the very edge of visibility, and be ready to veer off and temporarily break contact if threatened. A lot would depend on the weather conditions on the day, but Kummetz expected his northern pincer would be able to close to within ten miles of the convoy before it was spotted. At that range, the light conditions were just good enough to permit accurate surface gunnery. So, he should be able to keep the enemy destroyers fully occupied, while the southern pincer closed with the convoy.

Given the forces available to him, it made sense to use *Admiral Hipper* to spearhead the northern pincer. She was faster than *Lützow*, and so was better suited to playing cat and mouse in the darkness. Then, if all went well, the near-defenceless convoy would run straight into the path of the

The biggest threat to the Arctic convoys in Norwegian waters was the battleship *Tirpitz*. Her sortie the previous July led directly to the premature scattering of Convoy PQ-17. That December though, she was on this mooring in the Faettenfjord near Trondheim, undergoing a self-refit. That meant she couldn't join Kummetz's cruisers for the sortie.

armoured cruiser and her accompanying destroyers. It was an excellent plan, but it wasn't foolproof. Communications would be a problem. Success depended on maintaining radio silence, so unless a U-boat was in the area, and able to send sighting reports of the convoy, neither pincer would be able to communicate with the other until the attack began. This also called for some near-perfect navigation, in an area where obtaining an accurate navigational fix was nigh-on impossible. In these seas, at that time of year, the often extreme weather conditions were another variable. Above all, despite the plan, Kummetz knew that, ultimately, success would depend on a healthy dose of luck.

Another troublesome factor was the German chain of command. In normal circumstances, this ran from *Grossadmiral* Raeder, the head of the German Naval Staff (SKL), through his Operations Division to Gruppe Nord, based in Kiel. Gruppe Nord incorporated all Kriegsmarine units in northern waters, and was commanded by *Generaladmiral* Rolf Carls. The next rung in the chain was *Konteradmiral* Otto Klüber, Flag Officer, Northern Waters, or *Admiral* Nord, Norwegian Waters. He was in charge of all naval forces in northern Norway. From him, the chain of command then passed down to Kummetz on board *Admiral Hipper*. This was a rigid command structure at the best of times, but for Operation *Regenbogen*, an additional factor was the involvement of the *Führer*, Adolf Hitler.

By that stage of the war, Hitler was, for the most part, based in his operational headquarters – the *Wolfsschanze* (Wolf's Lair) near Rastenburg in East Prussia (now Kętrzyn in Poland). Hitler insisted on approving any operation, and it couldn't begin until he had personally given the order. This meant that *Admiral* Theodor Krancke, the Kriegsmarine representative at the *Wolfsschanze*, had to issue the appropriate order to Raeder, which was then passed down the naval chain of command until it reached Kummetz. With orders having to be encoded and then decoded at every stage, this made the whole procedure extremely cumbersome.

As if this wasn't enough, after the loss of *Graf Spee* and *Bismarck*, Hitler was averse to unnecessary risk in naval operations. It didn't look good on the world stage. So, he imposed a set of overly cautious standing orders governing the exposure of naval forces to undue risk. Kummetz might have had an extremely workable plan, but while his attack was being carried out he would have had to bear in mind Hitler's orders, and avoid any actions which might have placed his major warships in unnecessary danger. All naval actions involved risk, but Hitler's orders were clear: if faced by opponents of similar strength, Kummetz had to break off the fight. The result was that Kummetz lacked the freedom of action he required to press home his attack if faced with anything more powerful than a half-flotilla of enemy destroyers.

THE ROYAL NAVY

The biggest problem facing Admiral Tovey, commander-in-chief of the Home Fleet, was a lack of ships. In September, on its leg from Iceland to Archangel, Convoy PQ-18 had been made up of over 40 merchant ships, protected by almost 60 Allied warships, ranging from battleships to anti-submarine trawlers. That didn't even include the Soviet destroyers charged with guiding them into the White Sea. In early November, Operation *Torch* – the Allied landings in North Africa – had required the diversion of considerable naval and mercantile resources. While many of the Home Fleet's warships which had taken part in the landings had returned to Scapa Flow, Tovey was still short of ships.

His solution was to reduce the size of the convoys. Instead of one convoy of more than 30 merchantmen sailing once a month, he suggested splitting them into two smaller convoys. These would sail about a week apart, which in theory would give his larger warships a chance to refuel in between, and so be available to cover both sailings, as well as any homeward-bound convoy that would set off at roughly the same time as one of the outward-bound ones. An added complication was that in Archangel and Murmansk, the unloading facilities were being stretched to the limit by these large convoys, as was the rail network which transported its cargo south through northern Russia. More importantly, Tovey argued that smaller convoys would be easier to control, less likely to be detected, and could be protected with fewer warships. The Admiralty agreed.

So, the next convoy would be split into two smaller ones, JW-51A and JW-51B, each made up of around 15 merchantmen. The decision made, the Admiralty began assembling the merchant ships, cargos and escorts, while in his flagship in Scapa Flow, Tovey set about organizing the venture. After

Winston Churchill once described the convoy route through the Arctic as 'the worst voyage in the world', due to the harsh conditions and the ever-present danger of attack. Here, British destroyers batter through heavy seas, on their way to Murmansk.

the loss of the light cruiser *Edinburgh* in May, Tovey was reluctant to allow his cruisers to operate too close to a convoy, where they were more likely to fall prey to U-boats. Ideally, he didn't want his valuable cruisers to go further east than the longitude of North Cape, but First Sea Lord Sir Dudley Pound insisted they screen the convoys all the way to Murmansk. So, Tovey was forced to accommodate this requirement in his plans.

The scheme he devised would actually set the scene for most of the later Arctic convoys. The first convoy, JW-51A, would sail from Loch Ewe in the north-west of Scotland in mid-December. Convoy JW-51B would depart from the same assembly point a week later. Both convoys would approach Iceland, before heading east towards the Barents Sea. A total of 24 warships would screen the first convoy. A western close escort would accompany it as far as the southern coast of Iceland, when an eastern escort would take over. It would serve as the convoy's close escort all the way to the Kola Inlet, the gateway to Murmansk.

A fighting escort of destroyers would join the convoy when it passed Iceland, and it too would accompany it all the way. A small cruiser escort, designated 'Force R', would cover the convoy too, but keep its distance unless it was needed. Finally, a distant covering force of battleships, a heavy cruiser and a screen of destroyers would venture to a point roughly midway between Jan Mayen Island and Bear Island, before turning back. It was

The crew of a British destroyer in Arctic waters, enjoying a rare patch of good weather. This though, increased the risk of air attack, and so the ship's AA guns are manned and ready. The ferocity of Luftwaffe air attacks during mid-1942 led to the cancellation of further convoys until the winter darkness rendered air attacks impractical.

there in case the Kriegsmarine sortied in strength.

The arrangement for JW-51B would be pretty similar. In fact, Force R, having refuelled in the Kola Inlet, would return to the Barents Sea, to cover the second convoy. The western close escort would remain the same too, having returned from Iceland to Loch Ewe in time to accompany the next convoy. Finally, the homeward-bound convoy, RA-51A, was scheduled to sail from the Kola Inlet on 30 December. At roughly the same time, JW-51B was expected to reach the longitude of Bear Island. RA-51A too had an eastern and a western close escort, with the changeover taking place off Iceland. Force R would screen it as far as Iceland, when two more cruisers took over. A fresh distant covering force would also be on hand to protect its passage, once it drew close to Jan Mayen Island. Finally, a screen of submarines was to be deployed off the entrance to the Altenfjord, to raise the alarm if the German surface ships put to sea.

This hugely complex operation involving three convoys and 55

Vice Admiral Bruce Fraser (1888–1981) commanded the Distant Covering Force deployed to protect Convoy JW-51B. However, he was constrained by his orders not to enter the Barents Sea. A year later he would do just that when his flagship stalked and sank the German battleship *Scharnhorst*.

warships had to be planned in meticulous detail, and coordinated with forces in both home waters as well as in Iceland and northern Russia. Gradually though, everything coalesced, and by the start of December, given the approval of the Admiralty, Tovey was ready to start the operation. He would lead the distant covering force protecting JW-51A and RA-51, but these ships would return to Scapa Flow to refuel in between. Vice Admiral Fraser, Tovey's deputy, would lead the distant covering force protecting the second convoy. Tovey would therefore coordinate operations from Scapa Flow until his flagship returned to sea on 31 December.

Command of Force R was given to the man commanding the Home Fleet's destroyers, Rear Admiral Burnett, while the fighting escort of destroyers for JW-51B would be under the control of Captain Sherbrooke, the new commander of the 17th Destroyer Flotilla. Each of these four commanders knew what was expected of them, and had developed their own plans in the event the Germans tried to attack the convoy. Tovey had sufficient faith in his subordinates to let them decide their own course of action. So, while the German commander was constrained by the caution of his superiors, the British commanders protecting JW-51B had the freedom to do what they wanted, as long as they fulfilled their primary goal of protecting the convoy. Both Burnett and Sherbrooke were aggressive commanders, and both would abide by the old maxim about attack being the best form of defence.

THE BATTLE OF THE BARENTS SEA

The 16 merchant ships that made up Convoy JW-51A slipped out of the protected anchorage of Loch Ewe on 15 December, then headed north towards Cape Wrath. With them were the three escort destroyers that would accompany them as far as Iceland, as well as the corvettes, trawlers and minesweeper which would go all the way to Murmansk. Three days later, as the convoy was almost within sight of the south-east corner of Iceland, the escort destroyers parted company, and the fighting escort of six destroyers appeared. The following day, 19 December, Force R joined them, consisting of the light cruisers *Sheffield* and *Jamaica*, and the destroyers *Beagle*, *Matchless* and *Opportune*. The same day, Admiral Tovey left Scapa Flow in *King George V*, accompanied by the cruiser *Berwick* and three destroyers. They would form the convoy's distant cover force.

The weather was remarkably clement for that time of year, which increased the chances of detection by German aircraft or U-boats. However,

In the Arctic during winter, accurate navigation was vital to the success of operations, but it was extremely difficult to achieve. The lack of daylight and clear skies, or even a visible horizon, often made position-taking impossible. So, navigators had to use 'dead reckoning', an estimated position based on course, speed and known weather conditions.

the near-constant darkness of the Arctic in mid-December cloaked the convoy from prying eyes, and it passed Bear Island without incident. On Christmas Day the convoy entered the Kola Inlet. It seems that this time at least, the Germans had been caught napping. The two cruisers of Force R had arrived in the Kola Inlet the day before, and having refuelled, they were preparing to go to sea again, to cover Convoy JW-51B's passage through the Barents Sea. Meanwhile, on 25 December Tovey's distant covering force arrived back in Scapa Flow. It would sit the next convoy out, but six days later it would return to sea, to screen the transit of the returning convoy RA-51.

JW-51A HEADS NORTH

On the evening of Monday 21 December, as Convoy JW-51A was passing to the west of Jan Mayen Island, 800 miles to the south, the next convoy was setting out from Loch Ewe. Over the previous week Captain Radcliffe RNR had done wonders, preparing his civilian charges for sea. There were 15 merchant ships in the convoy – eight American, three British, and two which were American owned but registered in Panama. There were also two British-registered tankers. For this convoy, its commodore, Captain Melhuish of the Royal Indian Navy (RIN), flew his flag in the British-flagged freighter *Empire Archer*. Together they carried over 2,000 vehicles (mainly American trucks), 202 tanks, 87 fighters and 33 bombers, all in crates, plus just over 24,000 tons of fuel, of which half was for the aircraft. They were also laden with over 54,000 tons of general cargo, mainly foodstuffs.

Once safely out into The Minch, the convoy formed up into four columns, spaced 1,000yds apart, with 1,000yds between each ship within the column. The local escort of three Hunt-class escort destroyers had just

Bulldog was the only B-class destroyer converted into a specialist anti-submarine vessel, and she would have been a useful addition to Captain Sherbrooke's fighting escort. She missed the battle though, as storm damage suffered off Iceland meant she had to return home for repairs.

returned from escorting the previous convoy as far as Iceland, but now they were making the voyage again, formed up ahead and on the flanks of the merchantmen. Then the convoy set off northwards, making a steady 8 knots. The escort would be relieved when it passed the south-east corner of Iceland. By the following afternoon, it was well to the west of Orkney, and steaming through increasingly rough seas. The destroyer *Onslow*, flagship of the 17th Destroyer Flotilla, had been in Loch Ewe for the pre-sailing briefing, and had then sped off ahead of the convoy to join her flotilla in the Seidisfjordur, the navy's forward base on the east coast of Iceland.

Also heading north were two reinforcements for Captain Sherbrooke, the destroyers *Achates* and *Bulldog*, which had just been detached from the Clyde Special Escort. By now though, the rough seas had built up into a violent storm, with howling winds in excess of 60 knots. Both destroyers tried to ride out the tempest, but during a lull on Wednesday 23 December *Bulldog* resumed her voyage prematurely, and paid the price. The storm picked up again, and the 50ft waves ripped open the destroyer's forecastle like a sardine can. She limped back to Greenock for repairs, leaving *Achates* to continue on alone. She finally reached the sheltered Seidisfjordur at 11.30 the following day – just in time to repair the damage the gale had wreaked on her topmast before putting to sea again as part of her new flotilla.

By then Convoy JW-51B was about 150 miles to the south-east of Iceland, and heading north. She too had suffered during the storm. The British freighter *Dover Hill* had shipped water into her machinery spaces and her boilers were damaged. She was forced to turn for home. The rest steamed on, and by noon on Christmas Eve, as *Achates* was dropping anchor off Seidisfjordur, JW-51B was to the west of the Faroes. That day, Captain Sherbrooke held a planning meeting on board *Onslow*, and laid out his aggressive plans in the event the convoy was attacked. The older destroyers *Achates* and *Bulldog* – now reduced to just *Achates* – would stick with the convoy, which would have increased its speed to 10 knots and altered course directly away from the German threat.

The *Achates* would lay smoke to cover its withdrawal, while the smaller warships of the close escort would do what they could to shield the merchantmen. That left *Onslow* and her four sister ships. They were well used to working together, and so they would harry the attacker as a team, to buy time for the convoy to make its escape. Sherbrooke knew that his torpedoes were one-shot weapons. Once they'd been launched, the threat they posed would have gone. So, he planned to use the threat of a torpedo attack as an extra tool in his arsenal, and would only give the order to launch a real one if the potential rewards justified it. That done, and after refuelling, the flotilla put to sea at 23.00.

Once clear of the Seidisfjordur the six destroyers formed into line abreast, so their radars could cover as much ocean as possible. They then set off towards the east, in search of the convoy. They found it at 13.30 on Christmas Day, 150 miles to the east. It had been scattered slightly during the gale, but the weather had abated during the night. So, the destroyers helped the three escort destroyers round up the stragglers before heading on towards the north. Later that afternoon the eastern close escort arrived, led by Commander Rust of the minesweeper *Bramble*. Once it had formed up around the convoy, the western close escort was detached by Sherbrooke, and it headed off to the Seidisfjordur to refuel. Meanwhile, the previous convoy, JW-51A, was dropping anchor off Murmansk.

Convoy JW-51B crossed the Arctic Circle a little before midnight, and the following morning, Saturday 26 December, the seas were calm, although it was bitterly cold, and the decks were covered in ice. The convoy was making 8½ knots, and by noon it had reached 68° 23' North, 6° 32' West, a point roughly 250 miles to the north-east of Iceland. This meant though, that they were now well within air range of German-occupied Norway. Some 550 miles to the west, or just two and a half hours flying time away, lay the airfield at Bodø, home to a squadron of Focke-Wulf FW-200 Condors – the Luftwaffe's best long-range maritime reconnaissance plane.

Meanwhile, 570 miles to the south, Vice Admiral Fraser's Distant Covering Force was preparing to leave Akureyri on the northern coast of Iceland. The previous one, covering JW-51A, had just returned to Scapa Flow the day before, and Tovey's flagship, *King George V*, was now back at her usual mooring off Flotta. Fraser had left there on 22 December. After his flagship *Anson* transited the Eyjafjordur, she, *Cumberland* and five destroyers or escort destroyers set a course towards the north-west, and crossed the Arctic Circle just after midnight on 27 December. Fraser intended to reach his patrol area to the east-north-east of Jan Mayen Island by the morning of Monday 28 December. While it lacked the range and endurance to linger there long, Fraser's Distant Covering Force was ready to intervene if the Germans sortied to the west, or if *Tirpitz* put to sea from the Trondheimfjord.

At noon on Sunday 27 December the Allied forces were all in play. Convoy JW-51B had reached 70° 48' North, 0° 22' West, a position 150 miles due east of Jan Mayen Island. Both the close escort and the fighting escort had formed a screen around the merchantmen, which were now making roughly 8 knots, heading towards the east-north-east. Fraser's Distant Covering Force was roughly 320 miles astern of it, making 14 knots and heading on a similar course. About 675 miles to the west of the convoy, Force R was just passing out of the Kola Inlet, and by noon the next day it would be halfway between North Cape and Bear Island. From there, Burnett planned to cruise

to the west until he made radar contact with the convoy, approximately halfway between Jan Mayen Island and Bear Island. He expected that would take place around noon on Tuesday.

He would then reverse course and steam west, keeping between the convoy and the Altenfjord. As he did so, and according to his standing orders from Admiral Tovey, he was to keep about 50 miles from the merchant ships, to avoid attracting any undue attention from German reconnaissance planes and U-boats. So, these complex but well-choreographed manoeuvres continued as the convoy drew inexorably closer to Bear Island, and the Barents Sea. The hope had always been that bad weather would screen the convoy from both U-boats and the reconnaissance planes of the Luftwaffe. However, unknown to the Allies, the convoy had already been spotted. On Christmas Eve, as JW-51B was still to the south-east of Iceland, the weather had calmed sufficiently for the Luftwaffe to put up its maritime patrol aircraft. At around 13.15 that afternoon, a FW-200 from Bodø sighted the convoy, but wasn't spotted herself. The news was duly passed on to Kummetz.

The British freighter SS *Daldorch* of 5,571 tons was built in 1930 for the British and Burmese Steam Navigation Company, and spent much of her pre-war days operating out of Rangoon. In late 1942, she formed part of Convoy JW-51B, and was laden with 264 vehicles.

Since then, no German aircraft or U-boat had spotted the convoy. However, there could be little doubt where it was headed. At that time of year the pack ice reached as far south as Bear Island. This narrowed the entrance to the Barents Sea down to about 225 miles. As it was expected that the Allied convoys would pass close to the island, and as far from the Altenfjord as it could, then the likelihood was that any convoy bound for Murmansk would pass along a route which ran from the east of Jan Mayen Island to the south of Bear Island. That far north, the near continuous darkness made search aircraft virtually useless. Still, as the Germans knew the likely route

a convoy could take, they could place U-boats in its path. In effect, it was a maritime bottleneck.

At noon on Monday 28 December the convoy was at 72° 35' North, 4° 20' East, 140 miles to the north-west of its last known fix, and almost at that halfway point between Jan Mayen Island and Bear Island. It was approaching the start of the bottleneck. At the same moment, the distant covering force was 50 miles to the south, having just reached its patrol area earlier that morning. Force R was far to the east, and due south of Bear Island. Sure enough, three U-boats were lying in wait for the convoy, between it and Bear Island. A U-boat could detect a convoy by eye, or by using the boat's hydrophones. Then, even though an attack run might not be possible, at least it would confirm the convoy's location, course and speed, and so give Kummetz the vital information he needed to launch Operation *Regenbogen*.

That afternoon though, the weather had deteriorated. Another gale was blowing in, this time from the north-west. The wind increased to Force 7, 8 during the evening, and icy snow squalls battered the ships. By the early hours of Tuesday morning, the seas had become so rough that the commodore reduced the convoy's speed to just 6½ knots. The merchant ships were all rolling heavily now, and ice became a problem too. If it wasn't cleared from the decks and superstructure it would make the ships more top-heavy and so more likely to roll – and even to founder. So, regardless of the brutal conditions, work parties did what they could to chip the ice away as the ships wallowed their way through the gale. It was worse on the British freighter *Daldorch*, where the crew struggled to secure deck cargo that had broken loose.

The same happened on the American-registered freighter *Jefferson Myers*, which had to heave to facing into the gale so her crew could reshackle the crates. As a result, she dropped astern of the convoy and lost it in the darkness. The storm continued throughout the morning. The convoy's noon position on Tuesday 29 December was approximately 73° 19' North, 11° 45' East. However, this was very much an educated guess, as without a clear sky and a visible horizon, it was impossible to take a position fix accurately. So, the whole convoy was working on an estimated position. That afternoon though, the gale abated, and visibility increased. On the *Empire Archer* a

The American-registered SS *Jefferson Myers* of 7,582 tons formed part of Convoy JW-51B. The 20-year-old freighter was laden with 'general cargo' – a mix of tanks, vehicles, war materials and foodstuffs, all destined for the Soviet Union.

British Matilda tanks on the quayside of Murmansk, having just been unloaded from an Allied merchant ship. The ships of Convoy JW-51B contained 200 British and American tanks, along with over 2,000 military vehicles and 120 aircraft.

worried commodore found that only nine merchantmen were still on station. That meant that five of his charges were missing. The destroyer *Oribi* and the ASW trawler *Vizalma* had also disappeared. The priority now was to find the stragglers before a U-boat did.

Commander Rust in the minesweeper *Bramble* was detached to look for them, while the other escorts rounded up their remaining scattered charges and continued on their way. At midnight, the convoy altered course again, to avoid getting too close to the pack ice around Bear Island, 70 miles to the north-east. Its new course was now 090°, or due east, at a reduced speed of 6 knots, to give the stragglers a chance to catch up. At the same time, Vice-Admiral Fraser's Distant Covering Force was 80 miles to the south-west, and heading in the general direction of Bear Island. Force R was a similar distance to the south-east of the convoy, between it and the Altenfjord. Burnett had detached his two destroyers at 08.00 that Tuesday morning, when he'd come within radar range of the convoy. *Matchlock* and *Musketeer* headed back to Scapa Flow. That meant his force was reduced to just the light cruisers *Sheffield* and *Jamaica*.

Another development that afternoon was the arrival of four Allied submarines off the mouth of the Altenfjord. They kept out to sea, well away from the German minefields which protected the fjord's entrance. A fifth boat belonging to the Royal Netherlands Navy had also been part of the force, but had to return to Lerwick with engine trouble. These boats all had their own assigned patrol areas stretching from the mouth of the Altenfjord to North Cape. Their job was to spot any German warships putting to sea from the fjord, and to report the sighting to their flotilla headquarters in the Holy Loch. That way, the sighting report would be quickly forwarded to all of the Allied commanders at sea beyond the Arctic Circle. The secondary mission of these boats – like their German counterparts – was to attempt a torpedo attack if they were able to. However, warning the convoy was their top priority.

THE FORCES CONVERGE

Although the gale died away during the night, visibility remained patchy due to frequent snow squalls. Also, of course, it was pitch dark all the time, apart from a brief spell of less than two hours on either side of noon, when the darkness gave way to a sort of Arctic twilight. Then, visibility was good enough to pick out a ship several miles away, if the squalls didn't get in the way. Still, darkness or not, the stragglers had to be found. Fortunately, Sherbrooke's destroyers, like *Bramble*, were fitted with surface search radar. A little before 01.00 on Wednesday 30 December, the American freighter *Chester Valley* and the ASW trawler *Vizalma* were located some way to the north of the convoy. Although in these conditions accurate navigation was nigh-on impossible, Sherbrooke's navigator estimated that the gale had pushed the convoy about 13 miles south off its intended course.

At 11.30, as the twilight improved visibility, two more ships were spotted eight miles away to the south. Sherbrooke sent the destroyer *Obdurate* off to investigate. These turned out to be two more of the missing merchant ships, which were ushered back into the fold by 14.00. By noon on Wednesday, the convoy's estimated position was 73° 27' North, 19° 35' East. That put it about 55 miles due south of Bear Island. Despite being blown off course, at least the stragglers were beginning to rejoin the convoy. With 11 merchant ships back in the convoy, and a twelfth located to the north, accompanied by a trawler, Commodore Melhuish felt it was prudent to pick up speed again, to avoid being such a juicy target for a German U-boat. So, at 14.20 he ordered the convoy to increase speed to 8 knots.

The British O-class destroyer *Obdurate* was the first British warship to engage the enemy, when she stumbled across three German destroyers shadowing the convoy. Her captain, Lieutenant Commander Sclater, immediately raised the alarm.

On the evening before the battle, *U-354* was detected by Convoy JW-51B's escorts, and was depth charged. She managed to evade her hunters though, and later surfaced to transmit another sighting report, outlining the convoy's course and speed.

What Melhuish didn't know was that a U-boat had already spotted them, and was preparing to launch her torpedoes. At around 09.40 that morning, the convoy had been detected by *U-354*, a Type VIIc U-boat commanded by *Korvettenkäpitan* Herschelb. She had left the 11th Flotilla's forward base at Narvik 11 days before, and had been cruising to the south of Bear Island with two other U-boats, hoping to spot a convoy. That morning his hydrophone operator picked up the sound of ships' screws, and after working out its course and speed, Herschelb shadowed it on the surface, keeping to the south-west of his prey. Shortly after noon he transmitted a sighting report to Narvik, reporting six to ten merchant ships in quadrant AB 6394, steering 100°. He described it as a 'Poorly secured convoy, protected by several destroyers and up to one light cruiser'. So, Convoy JW-51B had been sighted.

While the report was forwarded to *Vizeadmiral* Kummetz on board *Admiral Hipper*, it wasn't enough to allow the admiral to unleash his battle group. Instead, he bided his time, waited for more news, and consulted his superiors in Narvik, Kiel and Berlin. Even then, nobody could do anything without Hitler's approval. So, Herschelb kept shadowing the convoy while the Kriegsmarine's high command waited for more information. Meanwhile, just in case, Kummetz brought his battle group to three hours' readiness. As the afternoon wore on, he doubted there really was a cruiser attached to the convoy. However, if Operation *Regenbogen* was going to go ahead, then his ships would be ready.

Shortly after 16.30, Herschelb sent in another sighting report. This said the convoy was 'In quadrant AC 4189, widely spaced – lengthy zig-zags on a mean course of 080° – about 10 merchantmen, several destroyers – the one cruiser doubtful'. He added that the visibility was good, apart from brief snow squalls. About 90 minutes later, as the darkness allowed him to edge closer, he decided to launch a torpedo attack. He launched three of them from his bow tubes, but moments later the convoy altered course onto the next leg of its zig-zag, and the G7a torpedoes passed harmlessly astern of the merchantmen. So, *U-354* resumed her shadowing, from her new position off the convoy's starboard side. Visual detection was almost impossible in the dark, so Herschelb relied on the skill of his hydrophone operator.

Then, a little after 20.00, the same operator reported the sound of a contact approaching fast. It had to be a British destroyer. Herschelb crash-dived his boat and tried to sneak away under the surface, while his men braced themselves for the depth charges. In fact it was the destroyer *Obdurate*, whose radar had detected a possible U-boat on the surface. Lieutenant Commander Sclater's destroyer raced to the scene, and began dropping depth charges. She was soon joined by *Obedient*, whose sonar found nothing. The hunt went on for the best part of an hour before the destroyers gave up and rejoined the convoy. Undeterred, Herschelb waited a bit, and then surfaced, so he could send in another sighting report at 22.00. It read: 'From 20.30 forced underwater, depth-charged. Last convoy location – quadrant AC 4513, course 120°.' He added that visibility was 13 miles, and weather conditions were very good. By then though, a second U-boat, *U-626*, had located the convoy and was sending in reports as well.

The more southerly course reported by Herschelb was probably a result of the convoy's zig-zagging, but it now placed JW-51B well within reach of Kummetz and his battle group. Little did the U-boat crew know, but that afternoon it had had its moment of fame in the *Wolfsschanze*. The U-boat's sighting report had been included in Hitler's daily briefing, and the *Führer* had decided to sanction the sortie, after impressing on his naval aide, *Admiral* Krancke, the need for caution. So, thanks to Herschelb, Operation *Regenbogen* was about to get underway. In the Altenfjord, Kummetz had second-guessed his superiors, and at 14.00 he convened an operational meeting on board his flagship. All six destroyer commanders were there, together with *Kapitän* Hartmann of *Admiral Hipper* and *Kapitän* Stange of *Lützow*. Over the next hour, Kummetz laid out his plan for *Regenbogen*, and issued his orders.

After his staff navigator projected the convoy's likely course, Kummetz outlined his plan to stalk it from astern and then divide into his two groups. He intended to take advantage of the midday twilight to launch his attack, to give his gunners the best possible chance to see their target. Then, as he put it, 'The main objective is the destruction of the defensive force.' After that he planned to strike the merchantmen, using surface gunnery to immobilize as many of them as he could as quickly as possible. While the meeting was taking place, a message arrived from Klüber in Narvik, asking him when the operation could begin. So, Kummetz took that as the green light he'd been waiting for. He immediately ordered all eight ships to prepare for a departure at 17.00 – in a little under three hours time. Later that afternoon, the official order reached him, having worked its way down the Kriegsmarine's lengthy chain of command.

The same orders which launched Operation *Regenbogen* also re-emphasized the constraints Kummetz would be working under. It told him to 'Avoid superior enemy, otherwise destroy if in [suitable] tactical situation'. Then, amid the frenzied activity aboard *Admiral Hipper* and their consorts, the ship's engineer reported a problem. The cruiser's temperamental propulsion system was being troublesome again. A flange on the starboard condenser pump was faulty, which, if the starboard engine was used, could well force the engine to be shut down. Kummetz and Hartmann inspected the condenser for themselves, then, after giving the engineers an extra hour, decided to risk putting to sea, and leave it to the engineers to repair the pump. It also bought time for a missing tug to arrive, to help *Lützow* out of the fjord. Now though, the departure was set at 17.45.

By then, the latest sighting report from *U-354* had reached Kummetz, and after poring over the chart, he and Hartmann decided this would place them in an ideal attacking position for the following day, at the start of the Arctic twilight. So, the preparations continued. Before they could sail though, another cautionary note had arrived down the chain of command. This time it read: 'Exercise restraint even when enemy is equally matched, as cruisers should not take big risks.' Essentially, this meant if two enemy cruisers were present, Kummetz should break off the attack. This contradicted his previous instructions about 'superior force', and was a direct result, it appears, of the cautionary interference of Hitler in the operation. So, Kummetz had to carry out an attack in the dark, against an enemy whose exact strength was unknown, but wasn't allowed to risk any of his own cruisers.

With these confusing orders, Kummetz gave the order to raise anchor. At 17.45 precisely, the eight German warships freed themselves of the seabed, and began moving up the long, twisting fjord. It lay 32 miles from the

Although all of the cruisers and destroyers which took part in the battle carried radar, these were often not switched on, to avoid revealing the ship's position. So, much of the time it was up to the ship's lookouts to spot the enemy, as was the case that morning, when *Obdurate*'s lookouts spotted three German destroyers to port of them.

The German pincer plan

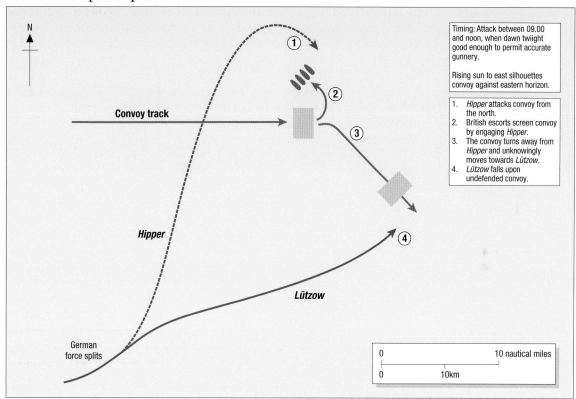

N

Convoy track

① ②

③

Hipper

Lützow

German force splits

④

Timing: Attack between 09.00 and noon, when dawn twiight good enough to permit accurate gunnery.

Rising sun to east silhouettes convoy against eastern horizon.

1. *Hipper* attacks convoy from the north.
2. British escorts screen convoy by engaging *Hipper*.
3. The convoy turns away from *Hipper* and unknowingly moves towards *Lützow*.
4. *Lützow* falls upon undefended convoy.

0   10 nautical miles

0   10km

open sea, so the transit was a lengthy one. Then, after clearing the island of Stjernøya, they began passing through the gaps in the defensive minefield laid across the western entrance to the fjord. It wasn't until 21.45, four hours after raising anchor, that the warships finally reached the open sea and were able to turn north into the Barents Sea, making 24 knots. At 23.00 he gave the order to turn onto a new north-easterly heading of 060°. After all, he planned to put off encountering the convoy until late the following morning. He knew that the success of the operation depended on a timely encounter with the convoy.

At that moment, Rear Admiral Burnett in Force R was roughly 330 miles to the north-east, having spent the day cruising well to the south of the convoy. Thanks to radio silence and the lack of a clear sky for navigation he wasn't certain where the convoy was. He knew that the convoy was due to pass south of Bear Island at 16.00 on 29 December, but the gale of the previous night may well have delayed it a little. In fact the convoy was well to the south-west of its expected position. At 18.00 that evening, Burnett's Force R was heading towards the south-west, and was probably well past the longitude the convoy had reached. So, at 18.00 he ordered his two cruisers to turn to port, and steer towards the north-west. It was a manoeuvre which would alter the course of the battle. Effectively, it placed Force R and the German battle group on what were almost converging courses.

That night, as Convoy JW-51B headed eastwards towards the same spot, after another ship joined him, Commodore Melhuish was still short of two stragglers, as well as the trawler *Vizalma*, last seen accompanying the freighter *Chester Valley*. *Bramble* was gone as well, out trying to round them up to the north-east of the convoy. So too was the destroyer *Oribi*, which also had a good-quality surface search radar. The rest of the convoy though, together with their escorts, pressed on through the night. The convoy was now making 8 knots on a base course of 090°. Kola Inlet, the entrance to Murmansk, was still more than 220 miles away, which meant that if all went well, then they'd probably arrive early on New Year's Day. That night Force R was close by, but would actually miss the convoy in the dark, and by morning would be to the north of it. Meanwhile, the German battle group was closing fast.

At 02.00 on Thursday 31 December – New Year's Eve – Kummetz's navigator placed their force at 71° 36' North, 24° 38' East. They were still making 24 knots, and it seems that the engine problems suffered by both *Admiral Hipper* and the destroyer *Z-31* had been dealt with. The German commander had already issued his orders, and his captains knew what was expected of them. At 02.40 they would split into two groups, with *Admiral Hipper* spearheading the northern pincer, and *Lützow* the southern one. At that moment, thanks to *Korvettenkäpitan* Herschelb, they had a better idea of where the Allied convoy was than most of the British commanders, and having just left the Altenfjord, their own dead reckoning was still accurate. So, Kummetz planned to use this information to place the southern pincer astern of the convoy during the early hours of the morning. The German plan, so carefully drawn up on paper, was now about to be put into practice.

THE NORTHERN PINCER CLOSES

When *Vizeadmiral* Kummetz drew up his plan of attack, he estimated that *Admiral Hipper* and the three destroyers accompanying her would reach 73° 40' North, 28° East at 08.00 that morning. At the same time, *Lützow* and her three destroyers would be 75 miles due south of him, and steering a course designed to reach the convoy around 11.00. By Kummetz's reckoning, that should place his flagship on roughly the same latitude as the convoy, and astern of it. A worrying development though, was the radio message from Narvik, passing on *U-354*'s last report at 20.30 the previous night. It put the convoy on a course of 120°, which was more southerly than he'd expected. This was probably a mistake, but that was a risk he couldn't take.

So, at 06.00 he detached his three destroyers, and ordered them to deploy to the south-east of him, and sweep towards the north. He also told them that if visibility dropped below seven miles, the destroyers were to switch on their radar sets for two minutes at a time, at ten-minute intervals. That way they had more chance of encountering the convoy, even if it was further to the south of where he expected it to be.

Another complication was a signal which arrived 15 minutes earlier, at 05.45. It came from *Admiral* Klüber in Narvik, having been passed on down the chain of command. For reasons that soon became apparent, *Kapitän* Stange of *Lützow* also received a copy. It read as follows: 'On completion *Regenbogen*, intending to release *Lützow* within the Barents Sea above 70° North, between 5 and 35° East. Mission: Cruiser warfare – detect enemy shipping, attack single cruisers and poorly armed escorts.' It went on to say that the success of *Regenbogen* was crucial to this new venture. It added

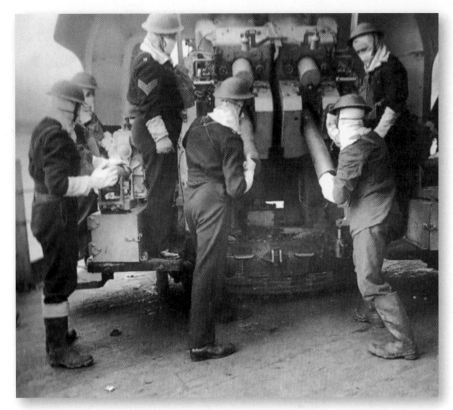

A British 4.7in. QF Mark XII gun and its crew, on the deck of a British destroyer. This was similar to the gun carried in *Onslow*, albeit she had single rather than twin-gun mountings. The rear of the turret was exposed to the elements, which in the Arctic often led to the freezing of the mechanism, as well to the discomfort of the gunners.

that *Lützow* would be detached from Kummetz's force when the codeword 'Aurora' was transmitted. It appears than neither Kummetz nor Stange had been consulted about this. *Lützow*'s captain had reservations, mainly because he lacked any forewarning, and didn't have a full picture of the operational situation in the Barents Sea. Just as importantly, he now needed to avoid any damage to his ship.

The timing could have been better. At that moment, the German battle group was about to launch its attack on an enemy convoy, and neither Kummetz nor Stange knew exactly how well defended it was. So far, all they had to go on were the often contradictory sighting reports from *U-354* and *U-626*, and an approximate course, speed and position for the convoy. Soon though, Kummetz would have more reliable evidence that the convoy was where he'd expected it to be. At 07.18, lookouts on *Admiral Hipper* spotted two darker shadows to the east-north-east, at the extreme range of visibility. The destroyer *Friedrich Eckoldt* was just within visibility range off the cruiser's starboard quarter, so Kummetz had a signal flashed to her, ordering her to go and investigate. The cruiser stayed on its present northerly course until 07.45, when Kummetz ordered her to turn to starboard, onto a new course of 090°.

With luck, if the sighting had been two ships from the convoy, then he would be to the north-west of it. His destroyers, led by *Friedrich Eckoldt*, were to the south-east, and probing towards the north. So, if the convoy was out there, he'd find it. He was rewarded by another sighting just two minutes later. The cruiser's lookouts spotted another even larger shadow in the darkness, to the east-south-east. When it disappeared again Kummetz ordered the cruiser to close with it. It was probably one of the larger

The foredeck of *Admiral Hipper*, viewed from her foremast. Directly behind her bridge is her forward gunnery director, topped by a rangefinder. Her two forward twin 20.3cm turrets were also fitted with their own integral rangefinders, which could be used if her main director was knocked out.

OPPOSITE
The small Flower-class corvette *Hyderabad* of the Royal Indian Navy formed part of the convoy's close escort. She was the first ship to detect the Germans, but her captain mistook them for Soviet warships, and so failed to raise the alarm.

merchant ships in the convoy – probably one of its two tankers, which had dropped astern of the others. The 8,032-ton British-registered *Empire Emerald* was in the rear rank of the convoy's second column, so she seems a likely candidate. A few minutes later, as Kummetz and Hartmann conferred, the lookouts reported seeing six more shadows, directly ahead of them.

There was no doubt now. They'd located the convoy. However, Kummetz had no desire to go directly onto the attack. Instead, as he'd laid out in his plan, he intended to wait until at least 09.30, when there was enough light for his gunners to see their targets clearly. So, he ordered *Admiral Hipper* to turn away again, and ordered the destroyers to hang back too, until he released them to begin their attack. By 08.00, using short-wave radio, *Kapitän* Stange reported that *Lützow* and her three destroyers were in position to the south of the convoy, and slowly approaching it. So, despite the mediocre visibility, lack of clear navigational positions and the relative complexity of the operation, the German battle group was poised to strike. All it was waiting for was for Kummetz to give the word.

Unaware of the threat, the convoy was continuing on to the east, making 8 knots and steering a base course of 090°. The 12 remaining merchant ships were arrayed in four columns of three ships. The columns were 1,000yds apart, and each ship in the column was 800yds ahead or astern of the others. So, the 12 ships formed a perfect box. The commodore in the *Empire Archer* was leading the second column. The flagship was something of a problem, as despite all the efforts of her engineers, she threw up thick black funnel smoke. This, in theory, made her easier than the others to detect. Of course, to the hydrophone operator of a U-boat, the sound of 20 ships in formation was even more distinctive. By then though, dawn was approaching. When it did, for a few fleeting hours, visibility could extend for up to 7 miles towards the north, and 10 miles to the south. However, frequent snow squalls swept over the sea from the west-north-west, which reduced visibility considerably.

Arrayed around the convoy were seven escorts – five destroyers and two corvettes. *Onslow* and *Orwell* were 1,000yds ahead of the first and fourth column, while *Orwell* was the same distance off the port beam of the convoy, with *Obdurate* stationed in the same position off the starboard beam. Bringing up the rear were *Achates*, 800yds astern of the rear of the first column, and the corvette *Hyderabad*, which was the same distance astern of the fourth column. Midway between these two escorts was the second corvette, *Rhododendron*. Finally, 3,000yds ahead of *Empire Archer*

was ASW trawler *Northern Gem*, which was using her passive sonar to hunt out any lurking U-boats.

It was *Hyderabad* that first sighted the Germans, at 08.20. From her position astern of the right-hand column of the convoy, her lookouts spotted what looked like the outlines of two ships passing from north to south, astern of the convoy. However, the corvette's captain, Lieutenant Hickman, disregarded them, as an hour before his radioman had passed on a message from the commodore which told the convoy to expect to see two Soviet destroyers later that morning. Unbeknown to Hickman though, the message had been wrongly decoded. It should have read two aircraft. As a result, Hickman never reported the sighting. So, it was ten minutes later, at 08.30, that lookouts on *Obdurate* saw the two ships too, on a bearing of 210°. This

The old A-class destroyer *Achates* was badly damaged by *Admiral Hipper* as she tried to screen the withdrawal of the convoy. Her crew fought a losing battle to keep her afloat, and she sank with the loss of 114 of her crew.

The Command and Information Centre of a British wartime destroyer. While most destroyer commanders fought their ships from the open bridge, by late 1942 the sophistication of radar systems encouraged a better coordination of information, to give the commander a better picture of the tactical situation.

time, they were correctly identified as destroyers. The news was duly relayed to Captain Sherbrooke in the *Onslow*.

At first, Sherbrooke thought these might be *Oribi* and *Bramble*, which had been detached the previous evening to track down the convoy's stragglers. Still, just to make sure, at 08.54 he ordered Lieutenant Commander Sclater to peel his destroyer away from the convoy and investigate the sighting. At that moment, *Obdurate* was off the starboard side of the convoy. So, Sclater turned hard to starboard, and increased speed to pass astern of the convoy, which continued on its present course. Sherbrooke was concerned, despite his hope that it might be the two detached escorts. So, he took the chance to order his crew to breakfast, in case they had to go to action stations. The minutes ticked by, and still there was no more news. The light was improving now, and from *Orwell*'s position off the convoy's port beam he had a reasonably good view to the west – the direction in which the mysterious ships were supposed to be.

By 09.20 *Obdurate* had looped round, and was now astern of the convoy, heading north. So far, Sclater hadn't spotted anything, but his lookouts were sure they'd seen two destroyers. So, he pressed on. Then, at 09.15, his lookouts spotted them. There weren't two destroyers – there were three of them, in line astern, about four miles off his port beam. He ordered an identification challenge to be flashed by signal lamp. Sclater too was still thinking they might be Soviet warships, but as the minutes passed he began to realize they might well be German. The question was answered at 09.29, when the leading destroyer opened fire. In fact the three ships were *Friedrich Eckoldt*, *Richard Beitzen* and *Z-29*, with *Kapitän* Schemmel's destroyer leading the formation. As soon as *Friedrich Eckoldt* opened fire, Sclater realized what he was facing. He turned his destroyer hard to starboard and sped away to the east, as the German shells fell around him. Seconds later, the other two German destroyers opened fire as well. This salvo of five 12.7cm shells from *Friedrich Eckoldt*, fired at a range of 4½ miles, marked the opening shots of the battle.

The trap is sprung, 08.30–10.30, 31 December 1942

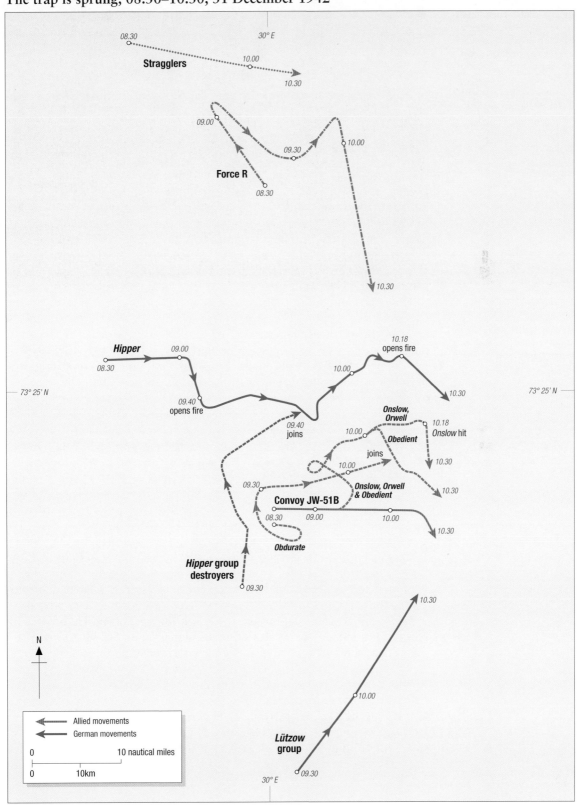

08.30
30° E
10.00
Stragglers
10.30

09.00
09.30
10.00
Force R
08.30
10.30

Hipper
09.00
08.30
73° 25' N
10.18
opens fire
10.00
10.30

09.40
opens fire
09.40
joins
10.00
10.00
**Onslow,
Orwell**
10.18
Onslow hit
Obedient
joins
10.30
73° 25' N

09.30
**Onslow, Orwell
& Obedient**
10.30
Convoy JW-51B
08.30   09.00   10.00
Hipper group
destroyers
09.30
10.30
Obdurate

09.30

N

10.30

10.00

**Lützow
group**

09.30
30° E

Allied movements
German movements

0   10 nautical miles
0   10km

CAPTAIN SHERBROOKE'S FIGHT

About 10 miles to the west, Captain Sherbrooke and the crew of the *Orwell* saw the flashes of gunfire through the gloom. Sherbrooke realized immediately that *Obdurate* had been fired on by the mystery destroyers, which meant they were German. So, at 09.31 he ordered his flagship to alter course to port, away from the convoy, and then to turn towards the north-west to investigate. As the *Orwell* turned onto her new course, Sherbrooke signalled *Obedient* and *Onslow* to join him. They too sped forward, turned to port to get clear of the convoy, and hurried after the flagship. So, within minutes of the *Friedrich Eckoldt* opening fire, three British destroyers were racing to intercept her. At the same time, Sherbrooke signalled to the *Obdurate*, ordering her to fall in astern of the rest of the flotilla.

He deliberately didn't order the *Achates* to leave the convoy, as her job was to protect it and the two corvettes. They were useful ships in an anti-submarine action, but in a gunnery battle they were little more than targets. *Achates* and the two corvettes began laying smoke, to screen the convoy, while the *Northern Gem* pulled back a mile, where she would be better placed to help the other escorts. Meanwhile, as *Obdurate* sped away, *Kapitän* Schemmel's three destroyers turned towards the north-east, as that was where he expected *Admiral Hipper* to be. At 09.30 she was actually ten miles to the north-north-east, heading east at 16 knots to place herself in the ideal firing position to engage the convoy. Of course, Kummetz realized that before he engaged the convoy, he had to neutralize the escorting British destroyers. That done, the merchantmen would be at his mercy.

At 09.40, when *Achates* at the rear of the convoy's port column began laying smoke, the mixture of white chemical smoke and black funnel smoke began to cloak the merchantmen. However, it also silhouetted the destroyer. The sharp-eyed rangefinder crew in *Admiral Hipper*'s forward fire control

A British destroyer laying a smoke screen, using the same methods employed during the battle of the Barents Sea. Chemical smoke dispensers fitted aft generate clouds of white smoke, while black smoke is produced through her funnel by altering the fuel–air mixture of her engines.

position spotted her, and the gunnery teams began their targeting calculations. *Kapitän* Hartmann turned his ship slightly to port so that all his main guns could bear, and within a minute of first spotting *Achates*, the cruiser opened fire under radar control. Her opening salvo of eight 20.3cm shells fell short, but within 15 seconds a second salvo was on its way. At that range – around nine miles – the shell's time of flight was 23 seconds. This time, the salvo straddled the target. On board *Achates*, Lieutenant Commander Johns had seen the cruiser's gun flashes, and tried to zig-zag to throw off the German gunners. It wasn't enough.

Although *Achates* hadn't been hit, shrapnel from near misses had punctured her hull, and killed or wounded several crewmen. It had also damaged the old destroyer's electrical circuits. More German salvos followed, causing more casualties, and adding flooding to the crew's problems. On *Achates*, the battle to stay afloat had begun, as damage-control parties tried to plug the shrapnel holes in the ship's side. The ship's doctor, Surgeon Lieutenant MacFarlane, busied himself dealing with the growing number of wounded being brought to his first aid post, while the dead were laid out in the wardroom. Still, Johns kept producing smoke, and worked his way back and forward at reduced speed, to make sure the convoy was thoroughly screened from the enemy cruiser, whose shells were falling dangerously close to the tanker *Empire Emerald*. So, for the moment, *Achates* was still in the fight, but it was only a matter of time before the German shells found their mark.

Suddenly, *Admiral Hipper*'s lookouts spotted another threat. At that moment, *Onslow* with *Orwell* astern of her were heading towards the north-west at 20 knots. At 09.34, *Obdurate* had sent a signal reporting: 'Three destroyers bearing 310°. My position 73° 36' N, 29° E.' So, Sherbrooke was expecting to encounter three large German destroyers, and his men were preparing for a gun action. Then, five minutes later, Sherbrooke's first lieutenant, Lieutenant Marchant, spotted another dark shape off the starboard bow, as it emerged through a snow squall. Sherbrooke immediately ordered the destroyers to turn towards her, and sent off a sighting report to all other Allied ships. It was eight miles away, and making a stately 10 knots. He thought she was a cruiser, but he couldn't be sure.

The *Onslow*'s gunnery director began tracking this new target, as the range steadily closed. Then, at 09.41, they saw the mystery ship turn slightly to port and open fire. Surprisingly though, the salvo wasn't directed at them. It roared past them, and fell close to *Achates*. It was at that moment that they realized they faced a German cruiser – probably *Admiral Hipper*, which Marchant reminded Sherbrooke carried eight 8in. guns. Unperturbed, Sherbrooke gave the order to open fire when within range. At that angle, 'Y' mount, the destroyer's after gun, couldn't bear on the target, and of her other three 4.7in. mounts, 'A' and 'X' were hindered by ice that was blocking the gun breeches. Firing semi-armour-piercing (SAP) shells, the guns had a range of just 6,500yds, or 3½ sea miles. *Orwell*, astern of her, had even less potent 4in. guns. For the moment then, all they could do was to close with the enemy.

It was a brave move, given the disparity in firepower. Of course, the destroyers carried 21in. torpedoes, four in *Onslow* and eight in the other O-class vessels. However, Sherbrooke was well aware that the threat they posed was every bit as important as the impact they might have if launched.

THE BATTLE OF THE BARENTS SEA: INITIAL CLASHES
09.00–10.30, 31 DECEMBER 1942

When *Vizeadmiral* Kummetz learned that Convoy JW-51B was entering the Barents Sea, he launched Operation *Regenbogen*. This involved splitting his force in two. A group consisting of the heavy cruiser *Admiral Hipper* and three destroyers would engage the convoy from the north, and attempt to draw off its escorts. It was expected that the now poorly protected convoy would turn away from this threat, and so Kummetz deployed his second group in its likely path. This southern group comprised the armoured cruiser *Lützow* and three more destroyers.

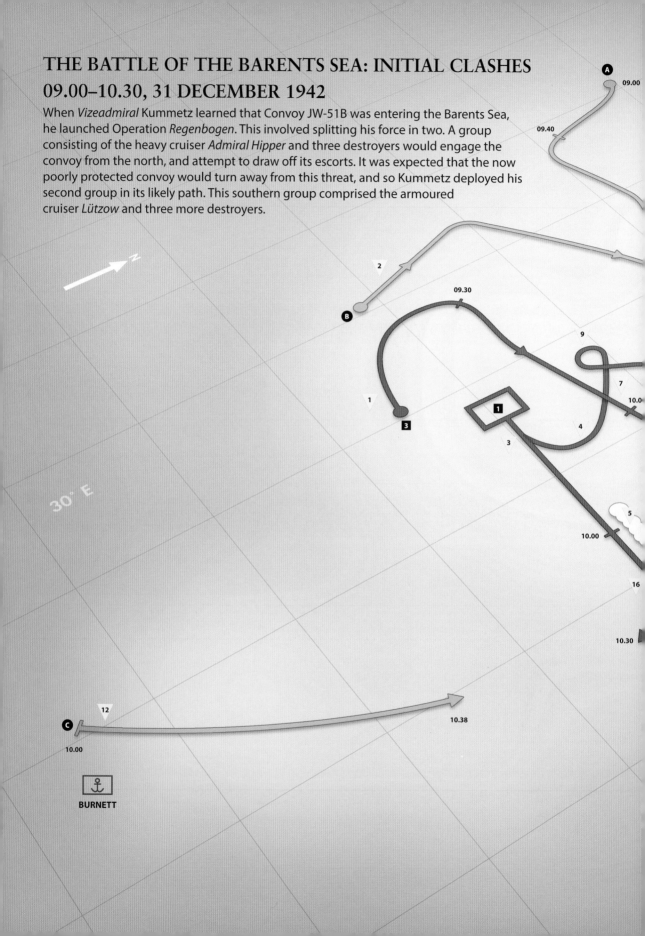

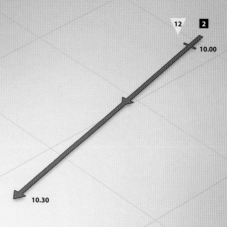

12 2
10.00

10.30

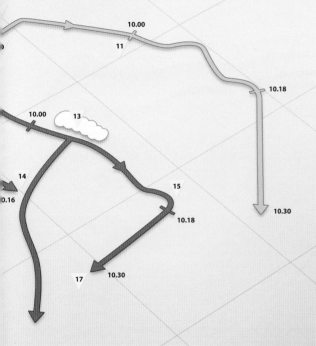

10.00
11
10.18

10.00   13
10.00   14
0.16   15
10.18
17   10.30
10.30

KRIEGSMARINE

A. *Hipper* group – heavy cruiser *Admiral Hipper* (flag, *Vizeadmiral* Kummetz)
B. Detached *Hipper* group – three destroyers – *Friedrich Eckoldt, Richard Beitzen, Z-29*
C. *Lützow* group – armoured cruiser *Lützow* (flag, *Kapitän* Stange) and three destroyers – *Theodor Reidel, Z-30, Z-31*

ROYAL NAVY

1. Convoy JW-51B (12 merchantmen, *Empire Archer*, flag)
    Close escort: two corvettes – *Hyderabad, Rhododendron*, one armed trawler – *Northern Gem*
    Ocean escort: four destroyers – *Achates, Onslow* (flag, Captain Sherbrooke), *Obedient, Orwell*
2. Force R – two light cruisers – *Sheffield* (flag, Rear Admiral Burnett) and *Jamaica*
3. Detached ocean escort: destroyer *Obdurate*

KUMMETZ

▼ EVENTS

1. 09.15: *Obdurate* sights and challenges three unidentified destroyers.

2. 09.30: *Friedrich Eckoldt, Richard Beitzen* and *Z-29* open fire on *Obdurate*.

3. 09.31: In *Onslow*, Captain Sherbrooke detaches the destroyer flagship from the convoy, and steams off to support *Obdurate*. Two minutes later, he orders destroyers *Obedient* and *Orwell* to join him. He also orders *Obdurate* to head towards *Onslow*.

4. 09.39: *Admiral Hipper* sighted by *Onslow*. Sherbrooke alters course towards her.

5. 09.40: Destroyer *Achates*, remaining with the convoy, makes smoke to cover its withdrawal.

6. 09.41: This draws the attention of *Admiral Hipper*, and she opens fire on *Achates*, damaging her with her second salvo.

7. 09.41: *Onslow* opens fire on *Admiral Hipper*. The German cruiser switches target and begins firing back.

8. 09.42: The three German destroyers rejoin their force flagship, and fall in astern of *Admiral Hipper*.

9. 09.44: *Onslow* circles to port, in an attempt to convince the Germans she is launching torpedoes.

10. 09.44: This ploy works, and *Admiral Hipper* turns away to the north.

11. 09.49: *Admiral Hipper* is obscured from *Onslow* by a snow squall. She reappears twice over the next 15 minutes to fire on the British destroyers before disappearing from view again.

12. 09.55: Rear Admiral Burnett, commanding Force R, signals to Sherbrooke that he is approaching him from the north. Meanwhile, *Lützow* group approaches the battle arena from the south.

13. 10.08: Sherbrooke detaches *Obedient* to reinforce the convoy escort, in case more enemy ships lie to the south. They lay smoke. *Onslow* and *Orwell* continue on to the east.

14. 10.16: *Obdurate* falls in astern of *Obedient*, and both destroyers now attempt to rejoin the convoy.

15. 10.18: *Admiral Hipper* opens fire on *Onslow* using her radar. Sherbrooke's destroyer is hit by two German salvos, and is badly damaged.

16. 10.20: The convoy alters course towards the south-east, directly away from the threat posed by *Admiral Hipper*.

17. 10.23: *Orwell* attempts to draw enemy fire, but both sides lose contact amid a snow squall.

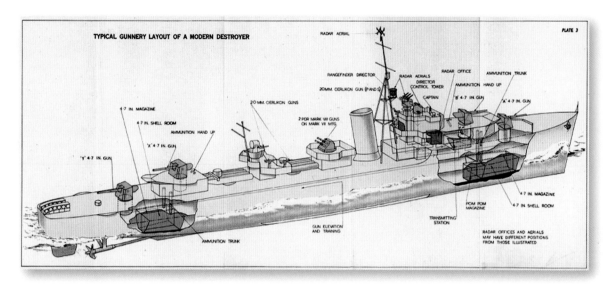

TYPICAL GUNNERY LAYOUT OF A MODERN DESTROYER

PLATE 3

RADAR AERIAL

RANGEFINDER DIRECTOR

RADAR AERIALS

RADAR OFFICE

AMMUNITION TRUNK

20MM OERLIKON GUN (P AND S)

DIRECTOR CONTROL TOWER

AMMUNITION HAND UP

CAPTAIN

'B' 4.7 IN. GUN

'A' 4.7 IN. GUN

4.7 IN. MAGAZINE

20 MM OERLIKON GUNS

4.7 IN. SHELL ROOM

AMMUNITION HAND UP

2 PDR MARK VIII GUNS ON MARK VII MTG

'X' 4.7 IN. GUN

'Y' 4.7 IN. GUN

4.7 IN. MAGAZINE

POM POM MAGAZINE

4.7 IN. SHELL ROOM

TRANSMITTING STATION

GUN ELEVATION AND TRAINING

RADAR OFFICES AND AERIALS MAY HAVE DIFFERENT POSITIONS FROM THOSE ILLUSTRATED

AMMUNITION TRUNK

This contemporary isometric drawing shows the typical weapons layout of a British war-built destroyer. *Onslow* though, had had her after torpedo tubes removed before the battle. When hit, fires beneath 'A' and 'B' gun mounts forced Captain Sherbrooke to order the forward magazines (shown here) to be flooded.

Once they'd been expended, then their potential threat evaporated. So, Sherbrooke decided to threaten a torpedo attack, in the hope that this might drive the cruiser off. By closing with the enemy cruiser, he might well make his opponent think he was moving in for a torpedo attack. Then, to distract the Germans even more, Sherbrooke gave the order to open fire. The bearing to the target had opened slightly, clearing the arc of 'Y' gun.

So, at 09.42, *Onslow*'s 'B' and 'Y' guns opened up. The two small SAP shells missed, but the two guns kept firing, while the crews of the other two mounts struggled to de-ice their guns. This certainly got the German gunner's attention, although so far the cruiser's guns were still trained on *Achates* rather than *Onslow*. Sherbrooke could see the three German destroyers now, about seven miles ahead of him, heading from left to right, as if to join forces with the enemy cruiser. However, snow squalls kept obscuring both the cruiser and the destroyers. It was 16°F that morning, or -9°C, but when those snow squalls hit the exposed gun crews it seemed even colder, especially as their speed – 24 knots – meant that it was like driving into a 30-knot ice storm. Although the destroyer's guns still hadn't scored a hit, at least they were engaging the enemy, and annoying them.

Meanwhile, as soon as *Onslow* reported sighting an enemy cruiser, on board the *Empire Archer*, Captain Melhuish warned the convoy and close escorts that he might well give the order to alter course to the south-east. In other words, he planned to head directly away from the threat, as soon as Captain Sherbrooke thought it was appropriate to do so. The escorts were still screening the merchantmen with smoke, and so far, apart from a few shells landing uncomfortably close to the *Empire Emerald*, the convoy itself hadn't come under fire. A few miles to the north-west, Sherbrooke noted that the smoke screen was largely obscuring the convoy from the enemy. By then, the German destroyers had reached *Admiral Hipper*, and Kummetz ordered them to fall in astern of him. They would come in useful if the British destroyers moved in to launch a torpedo attack.

That was exactly what Sherbrooke was planning to do. Rather he intended to give the appearance of carrying out a torpedo attack. So, at 09.44, he ordered *Onslow* to turn hard to port, followed by *Orwell*. He turned the destroyers in a full circle before settling on a north-north-easterly course, heading directly towards *Admiral Hipper*. Spotting *Obedient* closing fast from the direction of the convoy, Sherbrooke flashed the signal 'join me' to her. Meanwhile, both *Onslow* and *Orwell* were firing as they surged on, although so far they hadn't scored any hits. The range had dropped to four miles, or 8,000yds. The British 21in. Mark IX had a range of 10,500yds, and ran at 36 knots, but obviously the chances of scoring a hit improved as the range shortened. Ideally, to make his dummy torpedo attack look convincing, Sherbrooke had to close to within two miles. At any moment though, his destroyers could be torn apart by the cruiser's guns.

Although the range was decreasing, the German cruiser wasn't always fully visible, as the snow squalls kept obscuring her. Then, in between the squalls, the men on *Onslow*'s bridge saw the cruiser pick up speed, and turn away to port. *Admiral Hipper* turned directly away from them, until she was heading almost directly north. On board the German cruiser, the lookouts had spotted the British destroyers, but at first the ship kept firing at the more distant *Achates*. Now though, by heading towards him, these new British destroyers posed a much greater threat. To Kummetz, it looked like they were launching a torpedo attack. So, given his rules of engagement, his only option was to break contact. This was why the cruiser suddenly turned hard to port, and disappeared behind the line of snow squalls. Her accompanying destroyers did the same, and by 09.49 both sides were hidden from their opponents.

Sherbrooke called off the dummy attack, and altered course to starboard, until *Onslow* was heading due east. He'd realized that by closing with the Germans, he was being drawn away from the convoy. This way he could keep between the Germans and the merchant ships. *Onslow* reduced speed too, down to just 12 knots. *Orwell* and *Obedient* dutifully followed astern of her, each four cables (800yds) behind the destroyer in front. So far, Sherbrooke had held off the Germans, and prevented them from attacking the convoy. However, he realized that so far he'd been lucky. The Germans were still out there, and he was outnumbered and out-gunned. The next time she appeared,

The open bridge of a British destroyer was singularly unsuitable for operations in the Barents Sea in winter. Still, during the battle, commanders such as Captain Sherbrooke had to fight the battle from this exposed and freezing-cold vantage point.

Admiral Hipper could eviscerate his small force, which was all that stood between the enemy and the convoy. The only thing that could tip the balance in his favour was the sudden arrival of Force R.

Before these initial clashes began, Rear Admiral Burnett's two cruisers were 39 miles to the north. Force R had missed the convoy during the night, and instead, by 08.30, it was heading away from it, towards the southern edge of the pack ice. The two cruisers were in line astern, with *Sheffield* in the lead, and making 17 knots. His estimation of the convoy's position hadn't taken account of the fact that it had been blown southwards by the storm. Burnett kept on towards the north-west until 08.58, when *Sheffield*'s radio direction finder (RDF) picked up a low-frequency transmission to the north-west, roughly 7½ miles away. A few minutes later, the source was spotted on radar. It turned out to be two vessels – one large, the other small. By 09.06, the lookouts had spotted them – a merchantman and an armed trawler, heading east at 10 knots. It was *Vizalma* and her charge the *Chester Valley*.

Interesting though this contact was, it wasn't the convoy. So, Force R turned about, and headed off towards the south-east, in search of it. Thanks to this change of course, at 09.30 the cruisers were only a little further away from JW-51B than they had been an hour before. That was when lookouts spotted the flashes of gunfire on the southern horizon. It was the clash between *Obdurate* and the three German destroyers. Burnett altered course towards the north-east again, to check on the two stragglers before turning once more towards the south at 09.55. He was now steering 170°, and making a little under 30 knots. Burnett also signalled the convoy and Sherbrooke with the news that he knew roughly where the convoy was, and that he was steaming south to join them. For Sherbrooke this couldn't have been better news. All he had to do now was to keep the Germans at bay until Burnett arrived.

This meant that at 10.00, Sherbrooke's three destroyers were heading east in line astern, while the convoy was also on an easterly course, eight miles to the south-east. A fourth destroyer, *Obdurate*, was within sight to the south-west, and was slowly closing with him. *Admiral Hipper* and three German destroyers were somewhere to the north, just beyond visibility range, while even further to the north were Burnett's cruisers *Sheffield* and *Jamaica*, which were now racing to join him. At that moment the one element Sherbrooke wasn't aware of was that there was a second German group, which at that moment was about 18 miles due south of the convoy, and heading towards the north-north-east on a course designed to intercept it.

Even if the British flotilla commander didn't realize the danger the convoy was in, he must have felt uneasy at the way the convoy was so poorly defended. So, at 10.08, he ordered *Obedient* to detach herself from the flotilla, lay smoke and then rejoin the convoy. He sent the same signal to *Obdurate* too, which would fall in astern of *Obedient* eight minutes later. This was certainly a bold step, as at 09.57 and again at 10.04 *Admiral Hipper* briefly loomed out of the snow banks to the north and opened fire. Each time she fired four salvos at the British destroyers before slipping out of sight again. So, sending half of his flotilla away to reinforce the convoy was a calculated risk. Given what followed later that morning, it was a gamble that paid off. In the meantime though, that left *Onslow* and *Orwell* holding off a far more powerful and very elusive German force.

On board *Admiral Hipper*, *Vizeadmiral* Kummetz was experiencing a moment of indecision. He had been impressed by the way the British destroyers had been handled, and by the way Sherbrooke had prevented him from attacking the convoy. The use of a smoke screen had also effectively hidden the merchantmen from the German guns. His whole plan though, had revolved around the northern pincer drawing off the British escorts, and so leaving the convoy defenceless. So far this had worked, but thanks to the smoke screen he'd no real idea where the convoy was. The whereabouts of *Lützow* was also unclear, although he imagined she would fall upon the convoy from the south at some point over the next 30–40 minutes. Until then, Kummetz had been content keeping the enemy destroyers occupied. However, at 10.13 he decided to press the enemy harder.

Admiral Hipper turned onto a new south-easterly course, which should have brought her into visibility range of the four British destroyers. At the same time, he sent a signal which warned all German ships in his battle group that he was to the north of the convoy and that four enemy destroyers lay in between. His three destroyers were following the cruiser in line astern. Suddenly, at 10.18, the British destroyers appeared just over six miles ahead of them. As before, they were on an easterly course, so the range was closing steadily. As the cruiser's fire control team knew where to look, the main guns were already aiming in the right place, just forward of the starboard beam. So, it took less than a minute to make the fire control calculations, and unleash the first salvo.

At that range – about six miles – the time of flight was 13½ seconds. *Onslow* was the target – *Orwell*, five cables (1,000yds) astern of her, was left to the cruiser's secondary batteries, if they had a chance to open fire. At 10.19 the first salvo of eight 20.3cm shells fell a little astern of *Onslow*, between the two destroyers. The British destroyers fired back, but on board *Onslow* her two frozen guns still hadn't been able to join in. On 'A' mount, the crew was reduced to hammering the breech mechanism with shell casings in an attempt to get it to close. As the British fired, the German cruiser briefly swung away to port, but then swung back and unleashed a second salvo. This continued for another 30 seconds, with *Admiral Hipper* firing a third and fourth salvo. At 10.20 that fourth one achieved a perfect straddle

Although the destroyer *Onslaught* wasn't present at the battle, this view of her gives an excellent impression of her O-class sister ships which took part. All but *Onslow* carried three 4in. guns in single mounts, similar to the weapons shown here. Also visible on her foremast is her radar array, although at the time the ships of Sherbrooke's flotilla lacked the Type 285 fire control radar carried by *Onslaught* above her gun director.

THE GERMAN CRUISER *ADMIRAL HIPPER* ENGAGES THE BRITISH DESTROYER SCREEN, 10.18, 31 DECEMBER 1942 (PP.62–63)

Earlier that morning, *Vizeadmiral* Kummetz knew the convoy he was stalking was a few miles to the south of him. However, he delayed his attack until there was enough daylight for his gunners to see their target. By then though, the battle had already started, with British and German destroyers trading salvos in the darkness. Some 30 minutes earlier, Kummetz's flagship *Admiral Hipper* had briefly engaged the British destroyers, before breaking contact to avoid what the Germans thought was a torpedo attack. Three times during that half hour, the German heavy cruiser emerged from the cover of snow squalls to fire at the British destroyers.

Finally, at 10.18, she spotted the destroyer *Orwell*, and fired two salvos at her in quick succession. *Orwell* was badly damaged, with two guns knocked out, and 40 of her crew killed or wounded. She turned away, her decks ablaze, as *Admiral Hipper* slipped back into the darkness.

Here we see *Admiral Hipper* (**1**) firing a full salvo at the British destroyer, which lies five miles off her port bow. The fire of her eight 20cm guns is being directed from her fire control position (**2**), guided by information from her after radar (**3**), and her excellent optical rangefinders (**4**).

around *Onslow*. The destroyer had been successfully weaving between the shell splashes to throw off the German gunners, but this time her luck had run out.

The destroyer had turned hard to starboard in an attempt to dodge the German shells, but the salvo was perfectly placed, with shells landing in the sea on either side of the destroyer's bridge. When these detonated on striking the water, they showered the destroyer's superstructure with metal, cutting through the gunnery director behind the bridge. A jagged splinter of metal ripped into the left side of Sherbrooke's face, smashing bones and leaving his left eye hanging out of its socket. Another shell struck the destroyer behind the bridge, ripping her funnel apart and smashing her radar room, killing or wounding the operators there. High-pressure steam began streaming up through the hole in a spray. The ship seemed to stagger from these blows, but more was to come. Two more shells from the next salvo struck the foredeck, one exploding under 'B' mount, and the other a little further forward, near 'A' mount, where the crew was still trying to unjam its gun. Both guns were put out of action, as were most of their crews.

Despite being grievously wounded, Sherbrooke was still fighting his battered ship. He pressed the button to order the laying of white chemical smoke, and told the wounded helmsman to turn the ship to starboard. The next three German salvos fell harmlessly behind the *Onslow*. When the smoke began to hide the destroyer, *Admiral Hipper* turned her guns on the *Orwell*, following astern of her. She'd already been engaged by the cruiser's secondary 10.5cm guns, but so far she hadn't been hit. Having seen the havoc wreaked by the cruiser's main guns, her captain did the sensible thing and laid more smoke to cloak both destroyers from the Germans. He'd watched as *Onslow* had been hit, and later described how the destroyer had been

Under the command of Captain Sherbrooke, the O-class destroyer *Onslow* served as the flagship of Convoy JW-51B's fighting escort. During her fight with *Admiral Hipper* she was badly damaged, but she remained afloat, and so survived the battle. After being repaired in Rosyth, she returned to her duties in the Arctic.

swallowed up by clouds of smoke and steam, and he feared she'd blown up. However, when it cleared, the destroyer was still afloat.

Both destroyers limped away to the south, their guns silent, and the remaining crew of the *Onslow* trying to save their shipmates, and put out the fires that raged on board. For her part, *Admiral Hipper* continued on towards the south-west, and at 10.22 she ceased firing. The smoke screen had hidden the target, and then a series of snow squalls hid the smoke from sight too. On *Onslow*, Sherbrooke, miraculously still at his post, turned his ship beam on to the wind, to reduce the risk of the fires spreading. As damage reports came in, he realized just how badly shattered his ship was. He ordered the forward magazines flooded, as the fires around the foredeck were threatening to engulf them.

The shattered steam pipes had reduced propulsive power, but despite some flooding, *Onslow* was still afloat, and able to steam under her own power, albeit at reduced speed. Before he was taken below to be treated, Sherbrooke handed the ship over to Lieutenant Marchant, and told him to notify Captain Kinloch of the *Obedient* that he was to assume command of the fighting escort. Sherbrooke told his first lieutenant that as *Onslow* was too battered to fight, she should rejoin the convoy. That done, he placed himself in the care of the ship's doctor.

At 10.30, Kummetz ordered *Admiral Hipper* and her attendant destroyers to alter course to the north-east. He'd lost contact with both the destroyers and the convoy, so after disappearing from sight again, he planned to head east, to pull ahead of the remaining destroyers, and then to curve around to the south, in an attempt to locate the convoy. By now he expected *Kapitän* Stange to be drawing close to the convoy. What Kummetz didn't know was that the convoy was actually heading almost directly towards the southern German pincer. At that moment, unknown to both Stange and the convoy commodore, the two forces were just eight miles apart, with *Lützow* almost exactly due south of her quarry.

Having followed the course of the battle for the past hour, Convoy Commodore Captain Melhuish was well aware that the direction of the German threat had now shifted from the east to the north. First the sighting report from *Obdurate*, then its skirmish with German destroyers, followed by the appearance of a German heavy cruiser, had all shown a flow of battle around to the north-east. He still stayed on his present base course though, as he didn't have a clearer picture of how the battle was developing. However, the uneven duel between *Onslow* and *Admiral Hipper* had altered the whole picture. It seemed the cruiser was now due north of him. So, at 10.20, having forewarned his skippers, the commodore ordered the convoy to alter onto a south-easterly course. Then, once that had been achieved, he altered course again, and by 10.30 Convoy JW-51B was heading due south.

KUMMETZ SPRINGS HIS TRAP

What followed over the next 60 minutes was somewhat chaotic, involving several groups of ships, most of which had no idea where all of their own forces were, let alone those of the enemy. Essentially, at the heart of the action were the dozen merchantmen of Convoy JW-51B, which was heading due south at 8 knots, protected by two corvettes and a trawler. Astern of

Protecting the convoy, 10.30–12.00, 31 December 1942

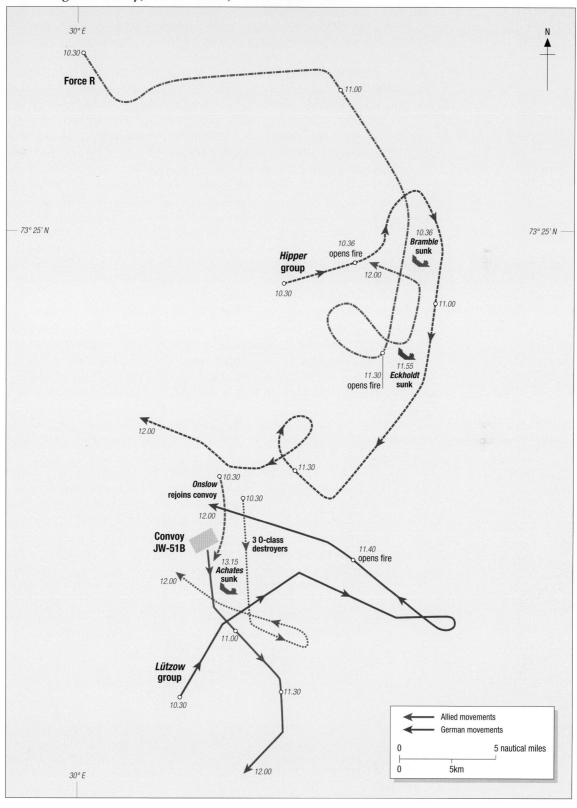

30° E

10.30
Force R

11.00

N

73° 25' N

73° 25' N

Hipper
group

10.36
opens fire

10.36
Bramble
sunk

12.00

10.30

11.00

11.30
opens fire

11.55
Eckholdt
sunk

12.00

11.30

10.30

Onslow
rejoins convoy

10.30

12.00

Convoy
JW-51B

3 O-class
destroyers

11.40
opens fire

13.15
Achates
sunk

12.00

11.00

Lützow
group

11.30

10.30

12.00

Allied movements

German movements

0   5 nautical miles

0   5km

30° E

them was *Achates*, bloodied but still in the fight, and still laying smoke. She was two miles astern of the convoy, while two miles off her port beam and also heading south were *Obedient* and *Obdurate*. They were making smoke too. On the far side of the smoke screen, two miles to the north were the badly damaged *Onslow* accompanied by *Orwell*. They were heading south too, protected by their own small smoke screen. Finally for the British, some 15 miles due north of these two destroyers was Burnett's Force R, advancing 'to the sound of the guns'.

As for the Germans, the northern pincer led by *Admiral Hipper* was now about five miles north-east of *Onslow* and *Orwell*, heading east at 30 knots, accompanied by her three destroyers. These German ships were hidden from the two destroyers by snow squalls. So too was another solitary British ship, the minesweeper *Bramble*, which was then about four miles to the north-east of *Admiral Hipper*. She was attempting to rejoin the convoy after searching for stragglers. About six miles due south of the convoy, the southern German pincer spearheaded by *Lützow* was on a north-easterly course, but hidden from the British by yet another even larger snow squall. The combination of smoke and snow squalls would add to the confusion of what was to follow, and result in some fleeting but deadly encounters.

The first of these clashes came at 10.36, when *Admiral Hipper*'s lookouts spotted a small warship off their port bow, heading away from them. Kummetz ordered Hartmann to engage her, and she opened up with both her main guns and her secondary ones. The Germans thought their target, just two miles away, was either a destroyer or a corvette. In fact she was *Bramble*, which had been attempting to rejoin the convoy. Presumably, Commander Rust had seen the flashes of guns, and was hurrying back to reinforce the convoy's escort. Instead, he ran straight into a German cruiser.

Inside the command and communications centre of a German Deutschland-class armoured cruiser. During his approach to the convoy, *Kapitän* Stange of *Lützow* had to rely on the flow of information gathered to reach the ideal position from which to engage the convoy.

He returned fire with his two 4in. guns, but it was an incredibly uneven fight. The Germans soon silenced her guns, and in a few minutes the minesweeper was crippled, ablaze and dead in the water. The German cruiser and her three destroyers swept past her, and at 10.43 Hartmann gave the order to cease fire as the snow hid the blazing wreck from sight. At 10.39, Rust managed to send off a sighting report on low-frequency, which was only received by *Hyderabad*.

At 10.46, Kummetz radioed *Kapitän* Schemmel in the *Friedrich Eckoldt*, ordering him to 'sink the destroyer'. He then ordered *Richard Beitzen* to accompany Schemmel. With that, the German flagship continued on to the north, followed by the destroyer *Z-29*. Four minutes later, he turned to starboard, and eventually settled on a southerly course. His intention was to relocate the convoy, and attack it from the north. By now, according to his calculations, it was about 16 miles away to the south, and *Lützow* should already be preparing to attack it. In fact, the convoy was further to the south-west than he thought, as it had changed course 20 minutes before. He was right about *Lützow*, though. The armoured cruiser and her three destroyers were indeed close to the convoy, and almost exactly where he expected her to be.

As the northern pincer had been stalking the convoy, the southern one had been advancing northwards, making 26 knots. At 09.30 they spotted gun flashes to the north-north-west, which suggested that *Admiral Hipper* was already in action. In fact, this was the initial clash between *Obdurate* and *Kapitän* Schemmel's three destroyers. Stange detached his three destroyers, hoping to locate the convoy, but they hadn't spotted anything, and by 10.30 they had rejoined the cruiser. In the meantime, they'd seen more intermittent gun flashes to the north, but the snow squalls effectively hid everything to the north of them from view. Then, at 10.42, they spotted the dark image of

The German armoured cruiser *Lützow*, which by late 1942 was easily distinguishable by her extremely high funnel cap. She began the war as the *Deutschland*, but Hitler changed her name, to avoid the propaganda setback if she was sunk.

a ship off their port beam. It might have been part of the convoy, or a British escort, but it was soon hidden behind a thick snow squall. So, defying orders, Stange decided to switch on his ship's surface search radar.

Three minutes later, this FuMo22 set detected several contacts off the cruiser's port quarter. This must have been the convoy. However, visibility was completely obscured by snow. Even if Stange did stumble across the convoy, he had no wish to run into any escorting destroyers when his own ship's gun directors would have been hampered by the poor visibility. He had no wish to be torpedoed at close range. He also didn't want to detach his own destroyers, as he would then find it difficult to control them when they disappeared from sight. So Stange decided to turn away from the contact towards the east, then work his way around the snow squalls. Then he would turn back, to fall on the convoy from the north-east, when he should have a clearer view of his target. He reduced speed to 12 knots, and at 10.55 he turned away to starboard, onto a new course of 120°.

Stange couldn't know that at about the same time the convoy altered course too, and was now coming round onto a south-easterly course, which it would stay on for another half hour. That meant that by 11.00, both *Lützow* and *Admiral Hipper*, as well as their destroyers, were to the east of the convoy, and were desperately trying either to locate it or to reach a position from which they could attack *Lützow*. At that point it was spotted by Lieutenant Commander Kinloch in *Obedient*. The destroyer had crossed the cruiser's wake amid the snow squalls, and was now five miles to the south-west of the German cruiser. So, *Kapitän* Stange had been right. Those radar contacts were the merchant ships of the convoy, while the first ship they spotted through the snow was probably *Obedient*, with an unseen *Obdurate* following astern of her. *Orwell* was also some way behind *Obdurate*, having watched the damaged *Onslow* take station at the edge of the convoy.

Kinloch ordered his three destroyers to turn towards the east, to keep between the German cruiser and the convoy. *Obedient* had now joined him, but *Lützow* and her destroyers – which Kinloch hadn't spotted – were now out of sight. He knew they were out there though, and expected they would return once they'd realized they'd steamed past the convoy. About six miles to the north-east, Stange was still slowly heading towards the east, away from the convoy. At 11.15 he decided to send Kummetz an update. It read: 'Enemy lost to sight'. This made little sense, as Stange undoubtedly knew where the convoy was. By rights he should have already turned to attack it from astern, but instead he held his course. The only explanation was his reluctance to place his ship in any danger, given the commerce raiding mission he was expected to begin as soon as *Regenbogen* was over.

Kinloch also sent a signal at 11.15. Given that he now knew he faced an armoured cruiser, he radioed *Achates* and ordered her to join him. Lieutenant Commander Johns replied that his speed was reduced to just 20 knots. So, Kinloch changed the order. *Achates* was to move to the head of the convoy and take *Orwell* under his wing. That way the two damaged destroyers could try to support each other. Tactically it made sense, but what Kinloch hadn't considered was the cover afforded by the smoke screen. As the convoy had changed course, the smoke now lay to the north-west of JW-51B. So, when *Achates* moved up towards the convoy, she emerged from the cover of the smoke. As she did so she was spotted by lookouts on *Admiral Hipper*. The cruiser was ten miles away to the north-east, and the destroyer would have been silhouetted against the whiteness of the chemical smoke. The cruiser immediately opened fire with her forward turrets.

The German fire was impressively accurate. The second salvo straddled the destroyer, and despite increasing speed and zig-zagging, *Achates* was unable to throw off the enemy's aim, and the next salvo scored a hit. The 20.3cm shell struck the destroyer's bridge, and utterly destroyed it, killing Johns and almost everyone on duty there. Lieutenant Peyton-Jones took command, and ordered course changes to the wheelhouse through a gaping hole torn in the deck. The destroyer was on fire amidships, and she was listing too, so presumably she was taking on water. The next two German salvos straddled the destroyer and damaged her boilers, reducing her speed to 12 knots. Mercifully, *Admiral Hipper* then ceased fire. Peyton-Jones couldn't know this was because she'd spotted the three O-class destroyers to the south, and had turned her guns on them. *Achates* limped away, hidden by smoke from the fires raging on her deck.

It was 11.26 when the British destroyers were spotted, and Kummetz immediately ordered the cruiser's gunners to switch targets. The cruiser had just turned to starboard, so she was heading towards the north-west, which meant all of her turrets could bear. The range was about 4¼ miles. In that light, the British destroyers were clearly picked out by the low winter sun. Just over two minutes later *Admiral Hipper*'s shells straddled *Obedient*, knocking out the destroyer's radio. By then, Kinloch had swung his line of three destroyers around, and he was heading to the north-west, to stay between *Admiral Hipper* and the convoy. However, he knew that *Lützow* was still somewhere out there to the north-east, and she remained a threat. Kinloch was in a very dangerous situation, and without a working transmitter

Convoy JW-51B was made up of ships like this – a variety of slow merchant ships, some newly built and others elderly. All were extremely vulnerable and lacked the damage-control facilities enjoyed by even the smallest of warships. So, when the Panama-registered freighter *Calobre* was hit by splinters, they damaged her boilers, and so reduced not just her speed, but that of the whole convoy.

THE CLIMAX OF THE BATTLE, 10.30–12.00, 31 DECEMBER 1942

So far, *Vizeadmiral* Kummetz held the advantage, and the attack was developing as he had planned. He decided to head south, to attempt to regain contact with the convoy. First though, he had to deal with a lone British minesweeper, on her way to rejoin the convoy after chasing stragglers. The minesweeper *Bramble* was hit repeatedly and sunk, and having detached two destroyers to hunt for more British strays, Kummetz ordered *Admiral Hipper* south. He was rewarded with a glimpse of the British destroyers, and quickly sank *Achates*. Minutes later though, the sudden arrival of Force R took him by surprise. *Admiral Hipper* was hit, and Kummetz ordered all remaining German ships to break off the action.

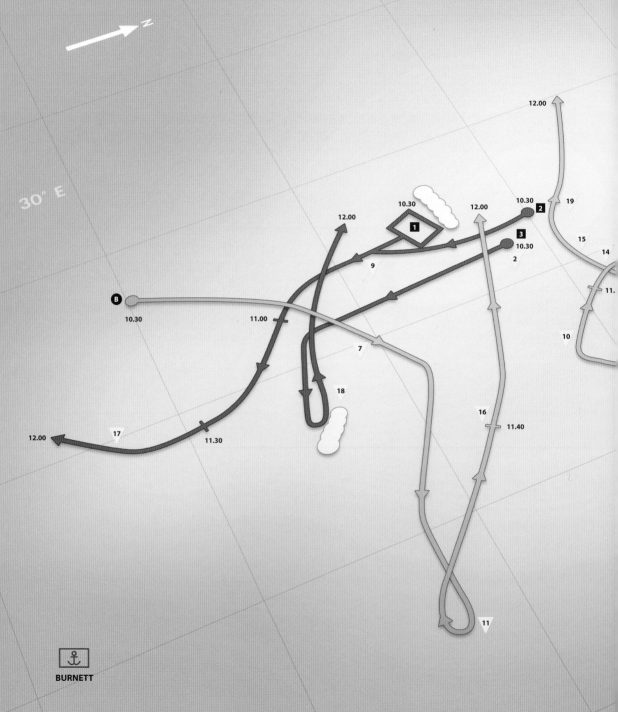

BURNETT

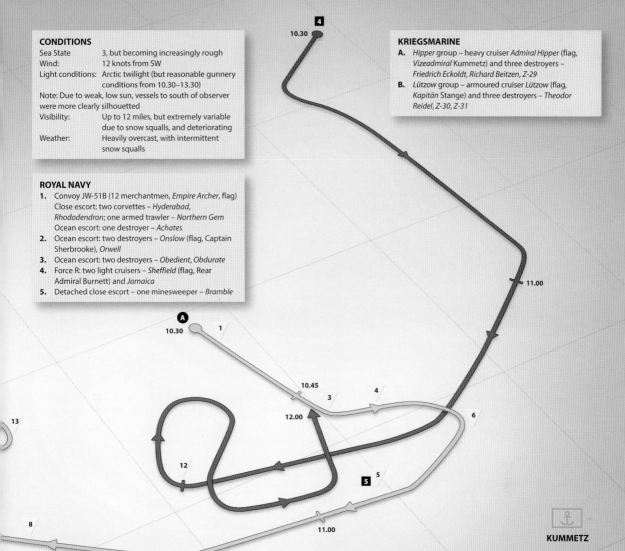

CONDITIONS

Sea State	3, but becoming increasingly rough
Wind:	12 knots from SW
Light conditions:	Arctic twilight (but reasonable gunnery conditions from 10.30–13.30)

Note: Due to weak, low sun, vessels to south of observer were more clearly silhouetted

Visibility:	Up to 12 miles, but extremely variable due to snow squalls, and deteriorating
Weather:	Heavily overcast, with intermittent snow squalls

KRIEGSMARINE

A. *Hipper* group – heavy cruiser *Admiral Hipper* (flag, Vizeadmiral Kummetz) and three destroyers – *Friedrich Eckoldt, Richard Beitzen, Z-29*

B. *Lützow* group – armoured cruiser *Lützow* (flag, Kapitän Stange) and three destroyers – *Theodor Reidel, Z-30, Z-31*

ROYAL NAVY

1. Convoy JW-51B (12 merchantmen, *Empire Archer*, flag)
   Close escort: two corvettes – *Hyderabad, Rhododendron*; one armed trawler – *Northern Gem*
   Ocean escort: one destroyer – *Achates*
2. Ocean escort: two destroyers – *Onslow* (flag, Captain Sherbrooke), *Orwell*
3. Ocean escort: two destroyers – *Obedient, Obdurate*
4. Force R: two light cruisers – *Sheffield* (flag, Rear Admiral Burnett) and *Jamaica*
5. Detached close escort – one minesweeper – *Bramble*

EVENTS

1. 10.30: *Admiral Hipper* turns to the north-east, having lost the British destroyers in a snow squall.

2. 10.35: Badly wounded, Captain Sherbrooke hands command over to Captain Kinloch of *Obedient*. *Orwell* is ordered to join Kinloch, and *Onslow* is ordered to rejoin the convoy. Kinloch's three remaining destroyers head south to better protect the convoy.

3. 10.36: *Admiral Hipper* sights the minesweeper *Bramble* ahead of her, and opens fire, damaging her badly. *Bramble* returns fire, but her gun is quickly silenced, and she sinks ten minutes later.

4. 10.40: Kummetz detaches *Friedrich Eckoldt* and *Richard Beitzen* to finish off the minesweeper.

5. 10.46: *Bramble* sinks with all hands. The two detached German destroyers remain in the area to search for further enemy ships.

6. 10.50: *Admiral Hipper* and *Z-29* turn south to relocate the convoy.

7. 11.00: *Lützow* group passes ahead of the convoy, but snow squalls obscure the protagonists. *Kapitän* Stange of *Lützow* decides to head east, in an attempt to locate the convoy.

8. 11.15: Kinloch orders damaged *Achates* to join him. As *Achates* turns to the west, she leaves the cover of her protective smoke screen, and is spotted by *Admiral Hipper*, which opens fire on her.

9. 11.18: *Achates* is hit and badly damaged. She is left dead in the water, and sinks two hours later.

10. 11.26: *Admiral Hipper* switches fire to *Obedient*, and straddles her within two minutes.

11. 11.27: *Lützow* group reverses course and resumes the search for the convoy to the north-west.

12. 11.30: Force R opens fire on *Admiral Hipper*, taking the German cruiser by surprise.

13. 11.31: *Admiral Hipper* makes smoke and turns to starboard, but is hit three times.

14. 11.34: *Admiral Hipper* returns fire, engaging *Sheffield*. However, she continues her turn, and Kummetz orders *Z-29* to lay smoke. Three minutes later, he orders all German ships to break off the action and retire to the west.

15. 11.42: While complying with this order, *Friedrich Eckoldt* and *Richard Beitzen* are sighted by Force R. *Friedrich Eckoldt* is hit repeatedly and left dead in the water. She finally blows up and sinks with all hands at 13.28. *Richard Beitzen* successfully breaks contact, and escapes to the west.

16. 11.42: *Lützow* sights the convoy, and opens fire. She damages the merchantman *Calobre*.

17. 11.43: The convoy responds by altering course to the south-west.

18. 11.45: The British destroyers alter course to north-west, and lay smoke to screen the convoy.

19. 11.49: *Admiral Hipper* sights the British destroyers and opens fire, straddling *Obdurate* before snow squalls obscure both sides.

KUMMETZ

73° 25' N

he couldn't control his flotilla. So, he handed over tactical command to Lieutenant Commander Sclater of the *Obdurate*.

It was 11.30. So far, despite the difficult weather conditions and the mysterious absence of *Lützow*, the battle seemed to be turning in Kummetz's favour. The convoy's destroyers were still putting up a fight, but they wouldn't last long in the face of two German cruisers and six powerful destroyers. Now, surely, the two German pincers would close, and the remaining destroyers would either be destroyed or be forced to withdraw. At that point the convoy would be at his mercy. Then, at that moment, everything changed. Without warning, the German flagship was straddled by a dozen shells. From the size of the large shell splashes, these weren't coming from a destroyer. Their new assailant was a British cruiser.

BURNETT'S ATTACK

Since just before 10.00, *Sheffield* and *Jamaica* had been racing south, as Rear Admiral Burnett knew that the convoy was under attack. A little over half an hour later he altered course to the east, when after the fight between *Onslow* and *Admiral Hipper*, he learned that the German cruiser was also heading east. He then turned to the south-east, and at 11.08 he was rewarded by a large radar contact which could only be *Admiral Hipper*. The German cruiser then turned south-west, as if heading directly towards the convoy. Burnett changed onto a near-parallel course. At 11.15 they heard firing ahead of them – the German flagship engaging *Achates*. They continued tracking the German ship, and at 11.26 the radar operators noticed she'd turned hard to starboard, and was steering towards the north-west. The range was down to eight miles. So, Burnett turned his ships to starboard, onto a parallel course, and gave the order to open fire. *Sheffield* opened up first, followed by *Jamaica*, which was 1,000yds astern of her.

The crew of *Admiral Hipper* were taken completely by surprise. It seems both their lookouts and their radar had let them down. *Sheffield* scored a hit with her second salvo. The 6in. shell penetrated the German cruiser's starboard hull just below the waterline, and detonated in No. 3 Boiler Room. The compartment was both flooded and on fire at the same time. Surprisingly, there was only one

One of the great advantages enjoyed by the British during the battle was radar. While the German warships carried radar sets of their own, these were markedly inferior to the British sets, in terms of range, definition and reliability. The British cruisers also employed highly accurate fire control radars linked to their main 6in. gun batteries.

fatality. *Kapitän* Hartmann immediately ordered the compartment sealed as soon as the engineers scrambled out, and the starboard engine was shut down. This reduced the cruiser's speed to 26 knots. Over the next two minutes, as both *Sheffield* and *Jamaica* engaged the German cruiser, *Admiral Hipper* suffered two more hits, starting a fire in her hangar amidships, and piercing her starboard hull. By then she was returning fire with her eight main guns, but smoke from her own fires hindered accuracy, and the salvos fell short. By now, Kummetz had realized he was under fire from a pair of British light cruisers.

In his report, the German admiral described what he decided to do next: 'I had to pull out of this unfavourable tactical situation … I therefore decided to pull all armed forces to the west, away from the battle area.' So, as *Admiral Hipper* circled to starboard, briefly steaming closer to Burnett's cruisers, he ordered Hartmann to make smoke to cover their withdrawal. The same order was passed to *Z-29*. The cruiser kept turning until it was heading away from the British cruisers, until it settled on a new south-westerly heading. Meanwhile, four miles to the north, Burnett also wheeled his cruisers away, as he was concerned the German destroyer he had spotted was one of several, and they planned to launch a torpedo attack. Unwittingly, this meant he was actually drawing closer to a pair of German destroyers – the ones detached almost an hour before, to finish off *Bramble*.

All this time the two German destroyers had been trying to rejoin the flagship. Schemmel exchanged radio messages with Kummetz, the last of which was sent at 11.42. It read: 'I can see a cruiser and a destroyer at 300°. Is that you?' In fact it wasn't – it was Force R. As *Sheffield* completed her turn to starboard she emerged on a reciprocal south-easterly course. At that moment, lookouts spotted a destroyer two miles ahead of them. It was *Friedrich Eckoldt*. The British cruiser opened fire, as Captain Clarke turned his cruiser to starboard, so all her guns could bear. Moments later, astern of her, *Jamaica* spotted a second destroyer, *Richard Beitzen*, a little

The German Type 36-A destroyer *Z-29* in 1945. During the battle she was ably commanded by *Korvettenkapitän* Rechel. She was retained by Kummetz when he detached his other two destroyers to finish off the damaged *Bramble*. So, she was spared the fate of her consort *Friedrich Eckoldt*.

THE BRITISH CRUISERS TAKE ON TWO GERMAN DESTROYERS (PP.76–77)

The short, sharp exchange between *Admiral Hipper* and Rear Admiral Burnett's two light cruisers was over in a matter of minutes, as the German ship broke contact behind the cover of a smoke screen. Sighting an accompanying German destroyer, Burnett ordered *Sheffield* and *Jamaica* to turn away, in case they launched torpedoes. As the two cruisers completed their circle to starboard, *Sheffield*'s lookouts spotted two more German destroyers almost directly ahead of them. They were just two miles away, and the leading destroyer, *Friedrich Eckoldt*, flashed a recognition signal at *Sheffield*, momentarily mistaking her for *Admiral Hipper*. *Sheffield* responded by opening fire on the German destroyer, while *Jamaica*, astern of her, opened up on the second destroyer, *Richard Beitzen*. She turned towards the

west, making smoke, while *Friedrich Eckoldt* turned to starboard, presumably to launch her torpedoes. Instead though, *Sheffield* turned onto a parallel course too, so all 12 of her main guns could bear on the destroyer. Within seconds, *Friedrich Eckoldt* was a burning wreck, and the threat she posed had been dealt with.

This shows the start of the exchange, with *Sheffield* (**1**) having fired her forward guns at *Friedrich Eckoldt* (**2**); the first of the cruiser's salvos has hit the German destroyer. Astern of the British flagship can be seen *Jamaica* (**3**); she will soon be firing at a target off her starboard bow – the destroyer *Richard Beitzen*. On the deck of *Friedrich Eckoldt* these first 6in. shells are having a devastating effect, causing at least two hits amidships (**4**) and around her bridge. The stricken destroyer would later sink with all hands.

over two miles off her starboard beam. *Fregattenkapitän* von Davidson of *Richard Beitzen* tried to warn Schemmel that these were British cruisers, but it was too late. At that moment, *Jamaica* opened fire too, but her target slipped away into a snow squall. *Kapitän* Schemmel though, was less fortunate.

His flagship was pounded by *Sheffield*'s 6in. guns – in fact by anything that could fire, including her 2pdr pom-poms. She was hit by *Sheffield*'s first salvo, and by the time the British cruisers swept past, the German destroyer had been fired on by 16 salvos and left a sinking, blazing wreck. Like *Bramble* before her, *Friedrich Eckoldt* was left alone in the darkness, as her crew tried in vain to save themselves and their ship. Consequently, nobody knows for certain when either ship finally sank. Firing to the north was heard from the British destroyers at 11.06. This may have been the German destroyer sending the minesweeper to the bottom, but in all likelihood *Bramble* sank with all hands half an hour earlier. At 13.28, lookouts on the British destroyers heard an explosion to the north-east, which may well have been the German destroyer blowing up. It is just as likely she sank within minutes of her encounter with *Sheffield*. In any case, she too went down with all hands.

As the guns on the British cruisers fell silent, a fresh round of firing erupted to the south. It was *Lützow*, which was belatedly firing her first salvo of the day. At 11.26, when Stange heard firing to the north-west, he realized the flagship must be engaging the convoy. So, he turned his cruiser to starboard, and faced towards the sound of the guns. At 11.42, he finally caught a glimpse of the convoy, nine miles away to the south. It was heading away from him, while three miles to the north of it was a line of three British destroyers, heading towards the east. Stange decided to ignore them for the moment, and to open fire on the convoy. She opened up with both her main and secondary guns, but ranging problems due to ice forced her 28cm guns to cease fire after their first salvo. However, several of her 10.5cm shells straddled the freighter *Calobre*, on the port side of the

The German destroyer *Richard Beitzen*, commanded by *Fregattenkapitän* von Davidson, survived her brush with the light cruiser *Jamaica*. Her sister ship and flotilla leader *Friedrich Eckoldt* was less fortunate, and was sunk with all hands.

THE GERMAN CRUISER *LÜTZOW* OPENS FIRE ON THE CONVOY, 11.42, 31 DECEMBER 1942 (PP.80–81)

At 11.37, *Vizeadmiral* Kummetz in *Admiral Hipper* ordered all his German ships to break off the action. The damaged German flagship then made smoke and sped off towards the west. However, some ten miles to the south-east the armoured cruiser *Lützow* was just about to fire her first salvos of the battle. A few minutes later her lookouts spotted the convoy, roughly nine miles away to the south. *Kapitän* Stange ordered his ship to open fire, and the salvo was accurate enough to damage the merchant ship SS *Calobre*, which was hit by shell splinters from a near miss from a 28cm shell. Then, three British destroyers appeared between *Lützow* and the convoy, laying a smoke screen which quickly hid the merchantmen from the German gunners. Stange ordered his men to cease fire, and the cruiser broke off the fight.

This shows the moment when the British destroyers *Obedient*, *Obdurate* and *Orwell* screened the convoy from sight, laying down a thick curtain of white chemical smoke, augmented by black funnel smoke (**1**). In the foreground the 28cm guns of *Lützow* (**2**) are shown still trained to the south, where the convoy is quickly being hidden from view. On the armoured cruiser's bridge (**3**), *Kapitän* Stange considers whether to switch targets to the destroyers, or whether to obey orders and speed after the flagship.

convoy, damaging her sufficiently with shell splinters that she pulled out of the formation.

On *Empire Archer*, the commodore immediately ordered his convoy to make an emergency turn away from the threat, onto a new south-westerly heading of 225°. On board the *Obedient*, three miles to the north, Lieutenant Commander Kinloch saw *Lützow* appear into view and open fire on the convoy. He reacted by ordering his three destroyers to turn hard to port, onto a parallel course to the German cruiser, and to begin laying smoke. At 11.45, as the white chemical and oily black funnel smoke began to obscure the convoy, *Lützow* ceased fire, and continued on towards the north-west, where Stange could now see *Admiral Hipper*. Four minutes later, a gap in the snow squalls meant that the lookouts on the British destroyers could also see both of the German ships.

The armoured cruiser was heading towards the west, so the British were five miles off her port quarter. Fearing they planned to launch a torpedo attack on *Lützow*, Kummetz ordered Hartmann to open fire. She straddled *Obdurate*, damaging her with shell splinters, but moments later another squall hid both ships from each other. With that, Kinloch ordered his destroyers to ignore the German cruiser, and to keep screening the convoy. As she sped away towards the flagship, *Lützow* also fired a few half-hearted salvos at the destroyers, before they disappeared from view. So far, the fighting escort had lived up to its name. It had fended off attacks by both German cruisers, and successfully protected the convoy. It looked like the Germans were breaking contact, and heading away from the merchantmen. They had suffered – both *Orwell* and *Achates* had been badly hit. Now, as the Germans sped away, the fight to save these two ships began in earnest.

Onslow was in less danger than *Achates*. Both ships were at the head of the convoy, and on *Onslow*, the flooding was less serious than the fires which were still burning. The worst was beneath 'B' gun, but at least with her magazines flooded there was little immediate risk of the ship blowing up. In the end, it was 14.30 before they were extinguished. The destroyer would

The poorly armed Halcyon-class minesweeper *Bramble* should really have stayed away from the convoy when her crew heard it come under attack. Instead, Commander Rust elected to rejoin it at the height of the battle, and consequently ran into *Admiral Hipper*. She was sunk with all hands.

THE PURSUIT: 12.00–13.00, 31 DECEMBER 1942

By now, both sides had lost contact with each other. However, both *Vizeadmiral* Kummetz and Rear Admiral Burnett knew roughly where at least part of the enemy force was. For Burnett, the most important thing was that the Germans were now heading away from Convoy JW-51B, and with twilight waning, it was unlikely the Germans would be able to relocate it. For him then, the plan was to pursue the Germans, to ensure the convoy's safety.

N

14

13.00

12.30

11

10

CONDITIONS

Sea State:	3–4
Wind:	12 knots from SW
Light conditions:	Arctic twilight (but reasonable gunnery conditions only until 13.30)
Visibility:	Up to 12 miles, but extremely variable due to snow squalls, and deteriorating

Note: Due to weak, low sun, until 13.30 vessels to south of observer were more clearly silhouetted

Weather:	Heavily overcast, with intermittent snow squalls

13

12.45

12.45

13.00

KRIEGSMARINE

A. *Hipper* group – heavy cruiser *Admiral Hipper* (flag, *Vizeadmiral* Kummetz) and one destroyer – *Z-29*

B. *Lützow* group – armoured cruiser *Lützow* (flag, *Kapitän* Stange) and three destroyers – *Theodor Reidel*, *Z-30*, *Z-31*

C. Detached from *Hipper* group – one destroyer – *Richard Beitzen*

ROYAL NAVY

1. Ocean escort: three destroyers – *Obedient* (flag, Captain Kinloch), *Obdurate*, *Orwell*

2. Force R: two light cruisers – *Sheffield* (flag, Rear Admiral Burnett) and *Jamaica*

13.00

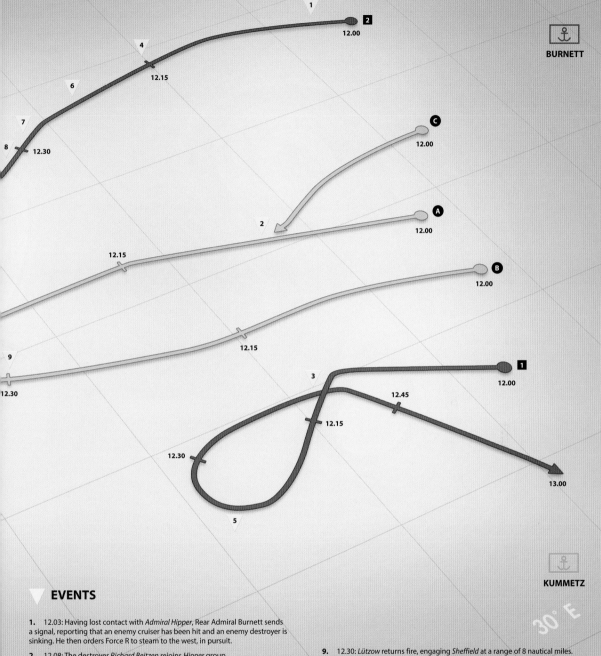

73° 25' N

1
2
12.00

⚓
BURNETT

4
12.15

6

7

8
12.30

C
12.00

2

A
12.00

12.15

B
12.00

12.15

9

12.30

3

1
12.00

12.45

12.15

12.30

5

13.00

⚓
KUMMETZ

30° E

▼ EVENTS

1. 12.03: Having lost contact with *Admiral Hipper*, Rear Admiral Burnett sends a signal, reporting that an enemy cruiser has been hit and an enemy destroyer is sinking. He then orders Force R to steam to the west, in pursuit.

2. 12.08: The destroyer *Richard Beitzen* rejoins *Hipper* group.

3. 12.10: Captain Kinloch alters course to the south-west, in case the Germans attempt to cut back towards the convoy.

4. 12.15: *Sheffield* briefly sights *Admiral Hipper* to the south-west, at a range of approximately ten miles.

5. 12.21: Having lost contact with the enemy, Captain Kinloch orders his destroyers to circle to the north, then return to the convoy.

6. 12.23: *Sheffield* sights the silhouettes of enemy destroyers to the south-west, at a range of approximately 12 miles.

7. 12.29: *Sheffield* opens fire on enemy destroyers of the *Lützow* group. However, initially they fail to spot the German cruiser, which is astern of the three destroyers.

8. 12.29: *Lützow* flashes a recognition signal at *Sheffield*, and is identified as a cruiser. So, *Sheffield* turns her guns on her. The German cruiser is straddled with the first salvo.

9. 12.30: *Lützow* returns fire, engaging *Sheffield* at a range of 8 nautical miles.

10. 12.33: Kummetz signals his superiors, reporting having lost contact with *Friedrich Eckoldt*, and that enemy forces are shadowing him. He also cancels the planned detachment of *Lützow* on an independent cruise.

11. 12.34: *Admiral Hipper* sights *Sheffield*, and opens fire on her, straddling Burnett's flagship with her first salvo.

12. 12.35: Finding himself targeted by two larger cruisers, Burnett orders Force R to cease fire and turn away to the north, temporarily breaking visual contact. Force R will continue to shadow the German ships using radar.

13. 12.40: Having broken contact with the British, both German forces continue to steam westwards, away from the convoy. Effectively, Operation *Regenbogen* has been aborted, and the battle comes to an end.

14. 12.45: To the north-east, Force R continues to shadow the withdrawing Germans using radar. Radar contact is finally lost at 14.00.

live to fight another day. However, the situation on board the *Achates* was much worse. She was listing heavily to port and the damage to her engines meant that speed was reduced to a crawl. She eventually lost all propulsive power. The list increased steadily, as did the amount of water entering the shot-riddled hull. As the trawler *Northern Gem* approached her she began to capsize. She lay on her beam ends for a while, before finally capsizing completely. Then she began going down by the bow. The gallant destroyer finally sank at around 13.00.

By noon, Rear Admiral Burnett's Force R had lost contact with the enemy. Instinctively he headed towards the west, and at 12.15 he was rewarded by a brief glimpse of *Admiral Hipper*, several miles to the south-west. By then *Richard Beitzen* had rejoined the flagship and taken up position astern of her. Four miles off the flagship's port quarter, *Lützow* and her three destroyers were making 26 knots, in an attempt to catch up. Meanwhile, to the south, the convoy was well out of reach of the German battle group, and its commodore had resumed his old easterly course. In *Obedient*, Kinloch kept his three destroyers together, acting as a screen between the Germans and the convoy. It was clear that the battle was over. All that was left was a pursuit.

At 12.23, lookouts on board *Sheffield* sighted four enemy destroyers several miles away to the south-west. Then, the cruiser's gunnery officer realized that the fourth destroyer was actually *Lützow*. Amazingly, the German cruiser thought *Sheffield* was *Admiral Hipper*, as she flashed her a

Gunners from *Sheffield*, after the battle, holding 6in. CPC shells of the type they fired at *Admiral Hipper* and *Lützow*. These shells, which weighed 112lb, were capable of being manually loaded by their crew for short periods, which gave a slightly higher rate of fire than if the normal automated loading mechanism was employed. This is exactly what these men did during the battle.

recognition symbol. *Sheffield* flashed one back, and then at 12.29 she opened fire at a range of eight miles, straddling the German cruiser with her first salvo. *Lützow* fired back, at which point Burnett decided her 11in. guns were more potent than his 6in. ones, and sensibly turned away. As *Sheffield* and *Jamaica* turned to starboard, they were spotted by *Admiral Hipper*. The German cruiser opened fire at 12.34, and straddled *Sheffield* with her first salvo. Burnett responded by turning away, and within a minute the two sides had lost contact with each other.

After that final salvo, Kummetz maintained a west-south-westerly course, with *Lützow* crossing the flagship's wake to take up position off her starboard quarter. For his part, Burnett turned too, onto a parallel course, where he could shadow the German battle group using his ships' radar. By then, Kummetz had already signalled Narvik, where his message could be passed on up the chain of command. He reported that he'd lost contact with *Friedrich Eckoldt*, and that he'd broken off the operation. He added that as British cruisers were shadowing him, he had also cancelled the planned detachment of *Lützow*. With that, Operation *Regenbogen* officially came to an end. Kummetz's signal though, disguised the real truth – that his German battle group had been driven off by lighter British forces, and the convoy itself was unscathed. When the real outcome of the battle became known, the operation would have consequences Kummetz and his men could never have imagined.

The light cruiser *Sheffield* carried her 6in. guns Mark XXIII in four triple turrets. These were similar to those mounted in the museum ship *Belfast*, and had a rate of fire of 6–8 rounds per minute – up to twice that of *Admiral Hipper's* 20.3cm guns.

AFTERMATH

Vizeadmiral Kummetz's battle group returned to the Altenfjord the following morning. Kummetz's plan had been a sound one, and it came very close to success. If the arrival of Force R had been delayed, or if either German cruiser had been handled more aggressively, then it was fairly certain that the remaining British destroyers and escorts would have been either sunk or forced to break off the action. The 12 merchantmen of Convoy JW-51B would then have been completely at the German's mercy. When he broke off the operation, Kummetz still had sufficient light to press home his attack, and to complete the job his men were there to do. Instead, his decision to withdraw had been forced upon him by his superiors. Effectively, he had been utterly hamstrung by the restrictions placed upon his actions. The need for undue caution, and his last-minute orders to avoid taking on an enemy of equal power meant that when Force R appeared, he had little choice but to break contact and call off the operation.

A similar degree of caution was imposed on *Kapitän* Stange of *Lützow*. That unexpected last-minute addendum to his orders – the need to carry out an independent commerce-raiding operation in the Barents Sea – was almost perfectly designed to hamper his own conduct of his ship. When he took

Hitler's fury at the Kriegsmarine's failure to destroy Convoy JW-51B resulted in the resignation of the fleet's commander-in-chief, *Grossadmiral* Erich Raeder (1876–1960). Here he is seen flanked by naval staff officers, in his Berlin headquarters.

on the convoy and its escorts that morning he knew he couldn't risk any damage to his ship, or waste too much ammunition. So, effectively, he was fighting the battle with these constraints in mind. It can be argued that Stange wasn't the most aggressive commander to begin with. These constraints though, limited his ability to fight. Then, when he'd worked his powerful ship into an advantageous position, he was given the order to break off the action and withdraw to the west. Therefore, the relatively poor performance of the German battle group that morning can be laid squarely at the feet of Kummetz's superiors.

When he learned of the battle, Hitler, still ensconced in the *Wolfsschanze*, was apoplectic with rage. Just the day before, he had railed at his naval adviser, Admiral Krancke, highlighting the superiority of the Royal Navy, 'which was able to sail through the Mediterranean without paying any attention to the Italian navy and Axis air forces'. In contrast, he described the Kriegsmarine 'as but a copy of the British and a very poor one at that. The ships are not in operational readiness; they are lying idle in the fjords, utterly useless like so much old iron.' Hitler never understood naval warfare, and the concept of a 'fleet in being', the very presence of which

Admiral Theodor Krancke (1893–1973) served as Hitler's naval adviser in the *Wolfsschanze*, and so he was the man responsible for breaking the unwelcome news of the battle's outcome to the *Führer*. Krancke was unable to mollify Hitler, nor prevent his decision to scrap the entire surface fleet.

tied down superior enemy resources, was one that he never seemed willing to grasp. He was, however, convinced that the Allies planned to invade Norway, and so earlier that year he had personally insisted that the Kriegsmarine in Norwegian waters was reinforced.

When Krancke first informed Hitler of the sighting of Convoy JW-51B, the *Führer*'s interest was piqued. He approved Operation *Regenbogen*, and then demanded regular updates on its progress. At the same time, he'd also reiterated the need for caution – a message which had been passed down the naval chain of command until it reached Kummetz. So, while Operation *Regenbogen* was a bold move, Hitler's insistence on caution, which had been reinforced by *Grossadmiral* Raeder, had effectively drawn the teeth from the operation before it had even begun. The added notion of sending *Lützow* on her own independent cruise after *Regenbogen* was completed had, apparently, come from *Generaladmiral* Carls, in command of Gruppe Nord. This last-minute change merely hampered Kummetz even further.

During the morning of New Year's Eve, Krancke dutifully kept Hitler fully informed of developments. So, he passed on the signal from *Kapitänleutnant* Herschelb in *U-354*, sent at 11.45, which said that the battle had reached its climax, and that he could only see red. This suggested the attack had been a success. Then, less than 15 minutes later came the signal reporting that Kummetz had broken off the battle. Even this sounded positive. As Krancke recalled afterwards, 'The *Führer* and I believed that in the main the attack on the convoy had come off according to plan.' That evening, a Reuters news report mentioned one German destroyer sunk and a cruiser damaged. Hitler demanded more information, but Krancke replied that due to radio silence, a detailed report would have to wait until Kummetz returned to the Altenfjord. Hitler became increasingly uneasy. However, in his live New Year address

Generaladmiral Rolf Carls (1885–1945) commanded Gruppe Nord, the Kriegsmarine's command that encompassed Norway as well as the Baltic. It was Carls who modified Kummetz's orders just as Operation *Regenbogen* was about to begin, ordering him to detach *Lützow* on a commerce-raiding cruise after the convoy attack was completed. This in turn hampered *Kapitän* Stange's handling of his ship during the battle.

to the German people, he claimed the Kriegsmarine had destroyed an entire Allied convoy.

Eventually, it was 19.25 on New Year's Day when Krancke received the news that an increasingly agitated Hitler had been impatiently waiting for. He had to tell his *Führer* that Operation *Regenbogen* had not been a success. He said, 'Our forces had been unable to penetrate the defensive screen of the enemy. While attacking the convoy from the north-west, *Hipper* had been engaged by the enemy's defence forces for a protracted period. She had been able to damage three to four destroyers. However, she ran … into gun range of an enemy cruiser. She was surprised and received damage … Commanding Admiral, Cruisers gave the order to break off the action and retire'. According to Krancke, Hitler had spent the day deriding the Kriegsmarine, saying, 'Its ships were utterly useless, that they were nothing but a breeding ground for revolution, idly lying about and lacking any desire to get into action.' To Hitler, this report fully underlined this lack of aggression.

At a meeting that evening, he vented his spleen at Krancke. First, he demanded *Grossadmiral* Raeder report to the *Wolfsschanze*. Then he continued railing at Krancke, yelling, 'This was typical of German Ships, just the opposite of the British who, true to their tradition, fought to the bitter end. He would like to see an army unit behave like that. Such army commanders would be snuffed out.' That evening he threatened to disband the Kriegsmarine immediately. As Hitler put it, 'This means the passing of the High Seas Fleet. It is now my irrevocable decision to do away with these useless ships.' After repeating this to Raeder on 6 January, he demanded a formal report from the *Grossadmiral*, explaining the Kriegsmarine's failings. Unable to criticize the constraints Hitler had imposed on it, Raeder could not satisfy his *Führer*'s anger, so he tendered his resignation. On 30 January he was replaced by *Grossadmiral* Dönitz, the former head of the Kriegsmarine's U-boat fleet.

In the end, Dönitz won a reprieve for the Kriegsmarine's surface fleet. Although the repair of *Admiral Hipper* as well as light cruisers *Emden* and *Leipzig* were deemed a low priority, the work on them continued, although it would drag on into late 1944, as resources were diverted elsewhere. The battleship *Gneisenau* wasn't so fortunate. Largely due to Hitler's wrath at the Kriegsmarine, her further repairs were cancelled, and her guns were removed to be used in coastal defences. *Tirpitz* remained in operation, at least until late September 1943, when she was put out of action during a midget submarine attack while lying in the Altenfjord. The Kriegsmarine's last operational battleship, *Scharnhorst*, was sunk in December 1943, not far from the site of the battle of the previous year. At that fight, known as the battle of North Cape, a newly promoted Vice Admiral Burnett played as important a part in the battle as he had done 12 months before.

Effectively though, Hitler's faith in the Kriegsmarine had been crushed by the battle of the Barents Sea. This action represented the German navy's last real chance to influence the course of the war. From that point on, it was regarded as the least important of Germany's three armed services, and instead its resources were diverted to the army and air force. While it maintained a presence in northern Norway, Hitler no longer believed it could influence the course of the war on the Eastern Front. That was now the task of the increasingly hard-pressed army. This also led to an increasing disregard for the service by the other arms of the German military. As a result, cooperation between the Kriegsmarine and the Luftwaffe, which had never been good to start with, now became virtually non-existent. Consequently, the remaining German warships in northern Norway were exposed to air attack – a development the British took full advantage of during their subsequent air campaign against the *Tirpitz*. Essentially, after the Barents Sea failure, with the exception of its U-boat arm, Hitler was prepared to abandon the Kriegsmarine to its fate.

Of course, for the Allies, the battle had been a tremendous success. A handful of British destroyers, supported by two light cruisers, had fought off a greatly superior enemy force, and had safeguarded the convoy. JW-51B would reach Murmansk on 3 January, while the following day *Oribi* would arrive, accompanied by the convoy's last straggler. *Vizalma* and her charge had rejoined the convoy on the day after the battle. While British losses had been significant – a destroyer and a minesweeper sunk – given the threat facing the convoy, this was a loss the Admiralty felt worth the price. As Admiral Tovey put it with some considerable understatement, 'That an enemy force of at least one pocket battleship, one heavy cruiser and six destroyers, with all the advantage of surprise and concentration, should be held off for four hours by five destroyers, and driven from the area by two six-inch cruisers, without any loss to the convoy, is most credible and satisfactory.'

British aircraft from the Fleet Air Arm, flying over the Kaafjord, the southern arm of the Altenfjord. This was the preferred lair of the German Arctic battle group, where it was well protected from attack by air or sea.

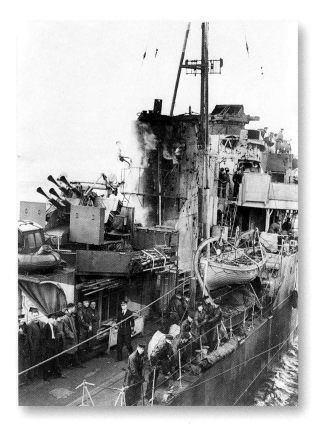

Both sides recognized the battle for what it was – a significant victory for the Royal Navy. While in the great scheme of things it wasn't much of a battle – merely a clash between cruisers and destroyers – its impact greatly outweighed everything else. From that point on, the Kriegsmarine's surface fleet no longer posed a significant threat to the Arctic convoys. Despite the presence of *Tirpitz* and then *Scharnhorst*, the convoys would continue, protected by an increasingly powerful Home Fleet, augmented by elements of the American Atlantic Fleet. When *Scharnhorst* did attempt a sortie, a year after the Barents Sea battle, she was cornered and sunk by British warships.

Inevitably, the battle was followed by a number of awards and promotions. Captain Sherbrooke was awarded the Victoria Cross, and after recovering from his injuries he remained in the service, before retiring as a Rear Admiral. For his handling of Force R, Rear Admiral Burnett was awarded the Distinguished Service Order (DSO), and the following year he would be promoted to Vice Admiral. Further DSOs and Distinguished Service Crosses (DSC) were given to several other participants, although all Commander Rust of *Bramble* or Lieutenant Commander Johns of *Achates* received were posthumous Mentions in Dispatches. The crew of *Orwell* were especially singled out, with seven more of her crew awarded the Distinguished Service Medal (DSM) for their actions in saving their ship. In the end though, the real beneficiaries of the victory were the people of the Soviet Union. Thanks to the efforts of these seamen, this vital lifeline of military aid would remain unbroken. Although this contribution wasn't fully acknowledged at the time, today, the Russian people fully credit the important part the Arctic convoys played in the ultimate defeat of Nazi Germany.

The destroyer *Onslow* after the battle. The damage to her bridge isn't readily visible here, but the shrapnel damage to her funnel and gun director are very evident. A total of 17 of her crew were killed during the battle, and another 23 injured.

The waters of the Barents Sea were incredibly inhospitable. It is estimated that a sailor whose ship sank would last up to ten minutes in those conditions. Those who were wounded would succumb far more quickly. This painting, of a wreath left by a U-boat, is a fitting epitaph for the crew of *Friedrich Eckoldt* and *Bramble*, both of which sank with all hands.

REMEMBERING THE BATTLE

A German wartime lament, popularized by U-boat crews, contained the lines: '*On a sailor's grave, no flowers bloom ... They have no grave but the cruel sea.*' This is particularly true for the men whose ships were lost in the Barents Sea that New Year's Eve. The entire crews of *Bramble* and *Friedrich Eckoldt* went down with their ships. The chances of surviving in those freezing seas were non-existent, and no friendly ship was on hand to pluck the survivors out of the water. To a lesser extent, the same was true for the crew of *Achates*. In her case though, 81 of her 194 crew were rescued by the other convoy escorts, spearheaded by ASW trawler *Northern Gem*, which doubled as a rescue ship. One of these survivors later died on board the trawler.

The dead of *Onslow* were buried at sea, while those of *Admiral Hipper* were taken back with her to the Altenfjord, and buried there. So, they were the exceptions – for the others, their ships became their tombs. Officially, the Admiralty reported the site of their sinking as 73° 18' North, 30° 06' East. In fact though, as subsequent seabed surveys have shown, all of the wrecks lay some distance from their last-known position. During the past two decades their locations have been tentatively identified during a series of thorough seabed surveys of the area, conducted primarily to determine the natural resources available beneath the sea. To date though, there has been no detailed exploration and survey of these three wreck sites. Instead, the remains of these warships have been left alone, out of respect for the seamen who were lost in them.

Although nothing marks the site of the battle, there are other legacies of the action. In Portsmouth, the Royal Naval Museum contains objects and documents which help tell the story of what happened that December, and the archive, together with that in the National Archives in London and the National Maritime Museum in Greenwich, contain a number of ships' logs, charts and records, all of which shed light on these events. The Imperial War Museum in London also contains a priceless recorded collection of oral testimony, some of which was given by British sailors who took part in the battle. The same is true of the Deutsche Marinemuseum (German Naval Museum) in Wilhelmshaven. Finally, although she took no part in the battle, light cruiser HMS *Belfast*, Vice Admiral Burnett's flagship at the battle of North Cape (1943), is preserved in the Pool of London as a historic ship. As a very similar vessel to Burnett's flagship a year before, and to *Jamaica*, she serves as a tangible link to Britain's wartime navy and the men who served in it during the battle of the Barents Sea.

FURTHER READING

Bekker, Claus, *Hitler's Naval War*, Macdonald & Jane's, London (1974)

Brown, David K., *Nelson to Vanguard: Warship Design and Development, 1922–1945*, Chatham Publishing, London (2003)

Brown, Peter C., *Voices from the Arctic Convoys*, Fonthill, London (2014)

Campbell, John, *Naval Weapons of World War Two*, Conway Maritime Press, London (1985)

Edwards, Bernard, *The Road to Russia: Arctic Convoys 1942*, Leo Cooper, London (2002)

Friedman, Norman, *Naval Radar*, Harper Collins, London (1981)

Friedman, Norman, *British Destroyers: From the Earliest Days to the Second World War*, Seaforth Publishing, Barnsley (2009)

Friedman, Norman, *British Cruisers: Two World Wars and After*, Seaforth Publishing, Barnsley (2010)

Gardiner, Robert (ed.), *Conway's All the World's Fighting Ships*, Conway Maritime Press, London (1980)

Gardiner, Robert (ed.), *The Eclipse of the Big Gun: The Warship, 1906–45* (Conway's History of the Ship Series), Conway Maritime Press, London (1992)

Gröner, Erich, *German Warships, 1815–1945*, Vol. 1, *Major Surface Vessels*, Conway Maritime Press, London (1983)

Heathcote, Tony, *The British Admirals of the Fleet 1734–1995*, Pen & Sword, Barnsley (2002)

Hodges, Peter, *The Big Gun: Battleship Main Armament, 1860–1945*, Conway Maritime Press, London (1981)

Hodges, Peter and Friedman, Norman, *Destroyer Weapons of World War 2*, Conway Maritime Press, London (1979)

Kemp, Paul, *Convoy! Drama in Arctic Waters*, Arms & Armour Press, London (1993)

Koop, Gerald and Schmolke, Klaus-Peter, *German Heavy Cruisers of the Admiral Hipper Class*, Seaforth Publishing, Barnsley (2014)

Koop, Gerald and Schmolke, Klaus-Peter, *German Destroyers of World War 2*, Seaforth Publishing, Barnsley (2014)

Mallmann Showell, Jak P., *Hitler's Navy: A Reference Guide to the Kriegsmarine, 1939–45*, Seaforth Publishing, Barnsley (2009)

Mallmann Showell, Jak P., *Swastikas in the Arctic: U-Boat Alley through the Frozen Hell*, Fonthill, London (2014)

Martienssen, Anthony, *Hitler and his Admirals*, Dutton Publishing, New York (1949)

Naval Staff History, *The Royal Navy and the Arctic Convoys*, Routledge, Abingdon (2007)

Pearson, Michael, *Red Sky in the Morning: The Battle of the Barents Sea 1942*, Airlife Publishing, Shrewsbury (2002)

Pope, Dudley, *73° North: The Battle of the Barents Sea*, Stratus Books (originally printed 1958), Looe (2013)

Roberts, John, *British Warships of the Second World War*, Seaforth Publishing, Barnsley (2017)

Roskill, Stephen W., *The War at Sea*, Vol. 3 (History of the Second World War Series), HMSO, London (1954)

Rueg, Bob and Hague, Arnold, *Convoys to Russia, 1941–1945*, World Ship Society, Kendal (1992)

Stephen, Martin, *Sea Battles in Close-Up: World War*, Vol. 1, Ian Allen, Shepperton (1988)

Whitley, M.J., *Destroyers of World War Two*, Arms & Armour Press, London (1988)

Whitley, M.J., *Cruisers of World War Two* Arms & Armour Press, London (1995)

Woodman, Richard, *Arctic Convoys 1941–1945*, John Murray Ltd, London (1994)

INDEX

Figures in **bold** refer to illustrations.